Another
Weird Year 2005

Another
Weird Year 2005

Huw Davies

cartoons by
Knife and Packer

TED SMART

First published 2004 by Ebury Press,
an imprint of Random House,
20 Vauxhall Bridge Road, London SW1V 2SA

Random House Australia (Pty) Limited
20 Alfred Street, Milsons Point, Sydney,
New South Wales 2061, Australia

Random House New Zealand Limited
18 Poland Road, Glenfield, Auckland 10, New Zealand

Random House South Africa (Pty) Limited
Endulini, 5a Jubilee Road, Parktown 2193, South Africa

The Random House Group Limited Reg. No. 954009

www.randomhouse.co.uk

Printed and bound in Great Britain by
Bookmarque Ltd, Croydon, Surrey

A CIP catalogue record for this book is
available from the British Library.

Typeset by seagulls

ISBN 0 091898366

Contents

Introduction

Welcome to this third incarnation of *Another Weird Year*, and the third introduction to a collection of the weirdest, stupidest, craziest and funniest news stories that have emerged during the last 12 months.

Someone – a cynic, clearly – once pointed out to me that I mustn't confuse change with progress. To begin with I wasn't quite sure what he meant, but he clarified by comparing computers with human beings. Computers have definitely progressed from the first vast mainframe machines that filled up whole rooms. The slender, light and compact laptop I'm writing this on is more than twice as powerful, twice as fast, twice as clever and 100 times more beautiful than the clunky, ugly, gas-fired desktop PC I wrote the very first *Another Weird Year* on. The same is largely true of most aspects of technology. Aeroplanes have progressed. Bicycles have progressed. And so on.

Humans. Now, he said, this is a whole other story. Humans evolved from apes, despite what a few idiotic creationists believe. And humans represent a kind of progression from the generations of apes that went before. Physiologically and psychologically, we are more advanced, adapted to a wider variety of conditions and climates. But, he told me, although humans have changed, and continue to change as we carry on shaping our environment, we have very definitely not progressed – only changed. We aren't any cleverer, any more compassionate, or less warlike. In some places, humans are more obese and have greater tendencies to certain illnesses, in other places they are fitter and healthier. Darwin himself (who? say the creationists) was keen to underline that when he talked about evolution, it was not to imply that any evolutionary stage was necessarily better than the last – it may have been better adapted to its environment, but it wasn't intrinsically better.

What on earth does this have to do with *Another Weird Year 2005*? It's just that as I've been collecting stories, reading huge numbers of what the world's media have offered up as examples of human weirdness, it strikes me that on the one hand things really do change, and that on the other things stay very much the same, which makes me think that my cynical friend – and Darwin – are right.

Take cleverness. There are still examples of positively Neanderthal stupidity popping up with disturbing frequency, often combined with highly evolved technology, as if to underline precisely that difference between change and progress. Like the man who tried to recharge his mobile phone in a microwave. Or the man who put petrol in his washing machine.

And anger. Stone Age man was probably far more peacefully inclined than the woman who broke her own legs with rage; or the woman who bit off another's finger at a party. In fact the 'Rage' section of *Another Weird Year* grows year on year, and throws up ever more unexpected types of rage than simple basic road rage: mayo rage, and spam rage, to name a couple, suggesting that modern man is a lot more angry than his prehistoric counterparts, who were never late for work, never got junk email offering to enlarge their genitals and were never kept awake by street musicians to the extent of having to shoot them, as happened last year. This category itself demonstrates that modern man will always get angry – no progress – but in a bewilderingly innovative variety of ways – change.

We may mock early man for worshipping trees and rocks, and believing in spirits in lakes and rivers. But there are no signs that we have progressed away from base superstition: believing that feeding your sick wife soup made with parts of humans is a good example that turned up last year, as was the story of the man making a charm against bullets who demanded that his client fire the gun at his head ...

The modern, sophisticated gourmet culture allows us to eat the finest – and most expensive – dishes that can be created, and to slap prepackaged, plastic food into the microwave for a meal in seconds. But we still find humans eating live worms, and toad soup, and even grass.

Just about any basic human attribute you can think of

is represented in *Another Weird Year 2005* in perfect, unprogressed idiotic beauty. So in the years to come, I look forward to no progress whatsoever in the human condition, just plenty of interesting change to give me more weird, wonderful and wacky stories to write up for you to read and enjoy. And if you do enjoy, and want to contribute a story or two of your own that you have come across, wander over to www.anotherweirdyear.com and jot it down for me.

Huw Davies
London 2004

Law & Order

ANOTHER CRIMINAL YEAR ...

We kick off with a look at some of the weird and wonderful criminal acts of the last year.

A woman was caught on CCTV stealing from an exhibition of medical antiquities in Kentucky. She walked off with 50 glass eyes, some bloodshot or jaundiced, so that they would match the wearer's other eye, worth a total of $2,500. Police regarded her crime as being somewhat shortsighted, since there is practically no demand for 100-year-old glass eyes on the black market. The woman's name? Melissa Wink.

He must have been taking the p**s – a man was arrested at a US airport after spitting what officials said appeared to be urine at security staff. The man was arrested at Charlotte Douglas International Airport, North Carolina, where witnesses saw the man take a sip from a container and then spit it on security screeners. The man was immediately wrestled to the ground and eventually taken to hospital. Maybe to provide a urine sample.

An illegal immigrant in Australia was caught and arrested at his place of work – a detention centre for illegal immigrants. The man had taken work as a sub-contractor and was sent on a job at the Maribyrnong Immigration detention centre in Melbourne. But when he got there, he was spotted by a visiting immigration officer who remembered the man's case and reported him.

A prisoner appeared in court in the US state of Texas, and because he was considered violent and a risk, he was fitted with a shock belt, a device remotely triggered to give the wearer an electric shock, stopping them in their tracks. True to form, as a woman who had been testifying against him left the witness stand, he launched himself forward to attack her; the judge frantically pressed the shock belt trigger, to no avail. After guards hauled him off the woman, who suffered minor injuries, they found that he had slid his lunchtime ham sandwich between the electrodes, rendering the belt useless.

In the Czech Republic a beggar took the trouble to dress up in green and cover himself with green ribbons, then to tell kids skating on a frozen lake in the city of Brno that he was a water nymph, and that unless they gave him his pocket money the ice would break. The police in Brno, who take a pretty dim view of water sprites begging, arrested him.

Another confidence trick, of a sort: in the town of Greenfield, Massachusetts, USA, a man reported buying a car. He opened the door to get into it, intending to sleep the night inside, and discovered three people already asleep inside the car – including the man who sold it to him.

A gunman burst into a classroom in the Maritime School in the town of Kotor in Montenegro, and forced teachers to give the pupils top marks in all their exams. The young man not only demanded top marks for all, but also insisted that the grades were set down in writing and passed on to the examinations board – and that he would return in a month to see that the grades were being honoured.

A German postal worker in the town of Gelsenkirchen started keeping packages rather than delivering them, then moved on to auctioning their contents on the eBay website. Before being caught, he had managed to sell over 100 items, for an estimated profit of about £13,000. Although the German Post Office were aware that stuff was going missing from his route, they were unable to prove anything until they received an official complaint from a musician waiting for a clarinet mouthpiece, who saw it on eBay, offered by the postman. Police searched his apartment and found the mouthpiece, as well as a vast amount of other packages.

CALORIE CRIME

A 68-year-old American health food executive was given a 15-month sentence for lying about his company's doughnuts. Robert Ligon's company labelled their 'carob-coated' doughnut as 'low-fat', showing on the label that each doughnut carried a mere three grams of fat, and just 135 calories. The truth, as his customers found, as their waistlines expanded rather than decreased, was very different. The fat fraud that Ligon had been committing was to buy regular full-fat, chocolate-glazed doughnuts from a commercial bakery and repackage them as 'diet doughnuts', before selling them on to diet centres. Analysis showed that these dietary deceptions had 18 grams of fat and 530 calories. And it was a nice little earner for the confectionery crook: he bought at around 30 cents a doughnut and sold them on for one dollar, making hundreds of thousands of dollars' worth of profit.

ODD

inadvertent crime

In Mexico, on the set of a low-budget film called *The Scorpion's Revenge*, actor Flavio Peniche was in a scene that required him to fire a gun at several people. He aimed his gun and started firing what were supposed to be blanks, but after two shots had rung out it quickly became apparent that the gun had been loaded with live ammunition. Actor Antonio Velasco had been shot, and was rushed to hospital where he died. Peniche was arrested, but freed on bail, while the police launched a search for the film's producer, Eduardo Sanchez, and a props manager known only as 'El Cepillo' (The Brush) who had disappeared after the tragedy.

SPUNKY CRIME

Arizona resident Tyrone Henry, 30, was motivated by God only knows what demons to pay women college students $10 to test a facial cream that he was producing. And I use 'producing' advisedly, since the cream that the victims rubbed into their skin while blindfolded was in fact his own semen. The authorities had great difficulty in classifying this as a crime, and ended up charging him with fraud. Henry asserted that he was breaking no law and was doing nothing more than pursuing the American dream (which in his case included selling photos of the blindfolded women with semen on their faces).

CAR-BASED CRIME

One of Mozart's greatest pieces of music is *The Magic Flute*. He was from Salzburg in Austria, which by coincidence is where this story's oddball is from. In the German town of Traunstein, close to the Austrian border, police were stupefied to see a man driving a car at 80 mph with both hands busy on the flute he was

Showing a highly developed sense of irony, an escaped convict in Germany was arrested when he was discovered posing as a police officer in the town of Bernau. Not just any old policeman, though. He had stolen a car, equipped it with a blue roof light and had been adding to his meagre income by carrying out routine traffic controls and taking on-the-spot fines from drivers. The man was wanted by police in Hanover, where he had absconded from home leave, and faced an additional sentence for his new crime.

playing as his car sped through traffic. The man was steering the car with his knees and feet while his hands were busy on the flute. He later told police that he wasn't actually playing the flute, just practising the fingerings.

Whereas a 54-year old man in Ontario, Canada, was not playing from imagination: a motorist was charged with careless driving when police caught him playing the violin at the wheel. The motoring violinist said he was warming up for a concert.

Meanwhile, a man was stopped for speeding near Toronto. It turned out that although he was driving too fast, he was cooking his dinner nice and slowly, in a slow cooker on the passenger seat – and tossing a salad to go with it too.

Carlos DeMarco of Parramatta, Australia, had been issued with two speeding tickets one after the other, having driven at over the 60 kph limit past the same speed camera twice. Fair enough. Frustrated at having been caught out, DeMarco went to find a 70 kph sign, tore it from its post, attached it over the 60 kph sign where he had been caught speeding, and took a photo of it. Brilliant idea. When he sent the photo, intended to prove his innocence, to court the judge was not taken in by the clumsy fake and gave him an extra fine of A\$1,000, to go with the A\$246 he already owed in speeding fines.

A driver in the American city of Seattle carried out a breathtakingly callous car crime. Troy Hagen, 29, was driving through the city in the early hours when he hit a man who had just come out of a nightclub. The victim was thrown up onto the bonnet of Hagen's car and head first through the windscreen. Hagen carried on driving, before stopping – not to see how his victim was, but to clear him out of his windscreen and dump his dead body onto the street. Hagen then drove for another 20 minutes through the city before his conscience finally got the better of him, and he reported the accident.

A pretty stupid car crime, this one. Rithcik Ramakri of New Jersey was driving along, and reading the speeding ticket he had just got. Which was why he ran into the back of an ambulance at a red light. No one was hurt, fortunately, but Ramakri got a dangerous driving ticket to go with the speeding ticket.

CAR-BASED NUDITY

When police in the German town of Huerth stopped a driver, they were astounded to find he was starkers, apart from a dog collar. And in response to being asked his name, the driver uttered no more than, 'Woof!' He was later banned from driving.

scaredy-cat car crime

Two Danish car thieves were so scared when they stole a car and then realised the furious owner was in red-hot pursuit that they called the police for help. The two men reported themselves and asked to be rescued at a nearby location.

BIZARRE

rabbit-poaching supercar

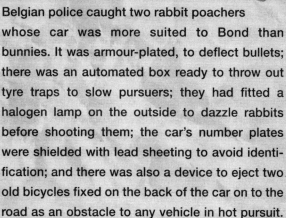

When you're on the trail of rabbits, you just can't have too much car. Belgian police caught two rabbit poachers whose car was more suited to Bond than bunnies. It was armour-plated, to deflect bullets; there was an automated box ready to throw out tyre traps to slow pursuers; they had fitted a halogen lamp on the outside to dazzle rabbits before shooting them; the car's number plates were shielded with lead sheeting to avoid identification; and there was also a device to eject two old bicycles fixed on the back of the car on to the road as an obstacle to any vehicle in hot pursuit.

TAXI-BASED CRIME

In the German city of Dresden two men got into a taxi one night and told the driver to take them to one of the city suburbs. When they arrived, one of the men produced a gun and ordered the driver to smear superglue over his steering wheel, then hold onto it. With the driver's hands tied, so to speak, the two men were able to take his wallet and make a getaway, ending up with a haul of several hundred euros. The driver was eventually freed by the emergency services.

NEARLY POINTLESS CRIMES

Petty crime doesn't get much pettier than these shabby, pathetic little efforts.

A 23-year-old man drove into a petrol station in Vermont, USA, and prepaid for $3 of fuel. Victor Cardoze then went back to the pump, daringly drew off petrol to the value of $3.50, pointed a gun at the station manager and roared off into the distance.

Combining pettiness with nuttiness, William Bresler attempted to rob a bank in Westerville, Ohio, of the sum of one cent, no more, no less. He was taken away for psychiatric tests.

In a supermarket in Arkansas, USA, Robert Boyer, 45, demanded to buy lettuce by the leaf and was refused. He took some lettuce leaves anyway, and walked out with them, only to find that he had committed his salad-based crime right in front of a police officer, who, also scoring highly on the pettiness scale, arrested him and charged him with robbery.

DOUBLE-CROSSING DOUBLE DEALERS

In Hanoi, Vietnam, one gang of crooks did a deal with another gang of crooks. Gang number one sold what it claimed was 'black bronze' to gang number two, for $40,000. Gang number two went off to resell the metal only to discover that it was nothing more than iron coated in cow fat. Meanwhile, gang number one went off to spend their money and discovered it was forged.

Talk about biting the hand that feeds you. A Chinese woman hired a hitman to do a job on her unfaithful husband's lover. She agreed a fee of 100,000 yuan (around £11,000) for him to kill or disfigure her husband's mistress, but he didn't go through with it. Enraged, she demanded her money back, but the hitman, plus a couple of mates, showed he did have the nerve to carry out a hit – he killed his employer.

This story is not so much about false-heartedness as false-breastedness. A farmer in eastern China paid £1,300 to wed a woman in an arranged marriage, and his new bride didn't sleep with him after the wedding because she felt ill. Before the week was out, she made a break for it, but the dogged farmer tracked her down to a neighbouring town and confronted her. They got into a clinch, and as they wrestled, a pair of false breasts fell out of the bride's clothing. He wasn't a she, and he had almost got away with his double-crossing scam; he was later arrested.

STUPID CRIMS

They still, stupidly, think they can get away with it ...

Another Weird Year has already featured the cashier in the USA stupid enough to accept a forged $200 bill that had George Bush's picture on it, the dimwit in question being blissfully ignorant of the obvious point that living presidents don't appear on banknotes. Well, it seems that the criminal genius who photocopied Bush's image onto some paper vaguely resembling money, and targeted a moron to use it on, struck again with his cartoon cash in the town of Roanoke Rapids, North Carolina. This time Michael Christopher Harris, 24, didn't find a dim enough recipient, and was caught and arrested.

In the US state of Washington, Trilane Ludwig was arrested early one morning and police gave his wallet to his mother, Angela Beckham, for safekeeping. A little later Ludwig asked his mother to pay his $500 bail using the cash from his wallet, but the cash was counterfeit, and so badly done – the banknotes weren't even the right size – that the pay clerk immediately noticed and the police were called in again. Ludwig remained in jail and his mother said she wasn't going to shell out any real cash to bail him out.

A man in Tennessee stole a fire department rescue boat and when he jumped overboard while being chased by the police he drowned. There were trained rescue personnel close by, but they could not go to his aid because their boat had been stolen.

Oh, what dreadful things can happen when you fail to keep a cool head and think for just one second. Nickolas Sandoval was changing a flat tyre by the side of the road in Texas when two police officers on patrol stopped to give him some help. Sandoval wrongly, paranoidly, and too hastily, assumed they had stopped because he had a bag of marijuana, and crammed it into his mouth to hide it, choking to death on it shortly afterwards. At least the police were there to take him to hospital.

Ben Rogozensky was halfway through a jail break when it went wrong in the worst possible way. Thirty-one-year-old Rogozensky, who was being held prior to his trial at a courthouse outside Atlanta, Georgia, decided to get away by climbing into the ceiling crawlspace. He made it away from his cell but then the ceiling collapsed, depositing him squarely into the judge's chambers – while the judge was there. His re-arrest was very swift.

STRANGE

A man was stopped by customs and excise men in Brunei after a high-speed chase, and was discovered to have smuggled into the country nearly 700 cans of beer. Mohamed Ali bin Hj Ibrahim was smuggling the beer in order to earn enough money to pay a £5,000 fine he had received two months previously. What had he been doing to incur the fine? Smuggling alcohol. He was fined £5,000. Wonder how he'll go about paying that fine ...

A teenager in the US state of Connecticut was arrested while trying to sell drugs to police officers. Not uncommon, but these were most definitely not undercover cops trying to ensnare dealers – they were on the lookout for fugitives and had jackets with the word 'POLICE' on them. Davaugn Goethe, 17, jumped into the back of their unmarked car and asked them what drugs they wanted. He even said that they looked as though they might be cops, but carried on trying to deal drugs to them. Goethe, who should have been in school anyway, was promptly grabbed and arrested.

ANCIENT CRIMS

A 91-year-old man from Texas admitted stealing about £1,300 from a bank – and it was his third robbery in under five years. 'Red' Rountree, who walks with a stick and is partially deaf, shuffled into a bank in

Abilene and gave a cashier an envelope with 'robbery' scrawled on it in red pen. Then he gave her another envelope, telling her to fill it with cash. The cashier asked him twice if he was joking, to which Rountree responded with threats of violence. So she let him get on with it, filled his envelope, watched him shuffle back to his car, while several people had the opportunity to note his car registration, and called the police as he was driving off. The police caught up with him not long afterwards, and he ended up with a sentence of 12 years in jail. And what are the odds on him serving his time, getting out and hitting the banks again?

In the German city of Essen, an 80-year-old man used a sledgehammer to break into a supermarket, by first breaking into an adjoining building, then using the sledgehammer to break through the wall into the supermarket. Not bad for an old-timer. He then carried on with his impressive display of strength and energy by filling eight shopping bags with food, mostly tins. Barely able to walk off with his loot, the man had not got far and was very swiftly arrested when the police arrived, after responding to the supermarket's alarm system.

ECONOMICALLY UNINFORMED CRIMS

Difficult to believe, this one, but a group of money forgers in Chile printed thousands of fake Argentinian banknotes – and made a loss. At the time the forgers made the counterfeit money, the Argentinian economy took a nosedive and the value of the peso sank so low that the police who caught the forgers were confident in stating that the cost of the special paper and ink would have been much more than the value of the notes they printed. The police spokesman added that the gang clearly didn't read the newspapers, and that they had to explain to the forgers that their fake money was worth three times less than its face value.

s-s-s-s-stupid crim

Staff at a bookmaker's in Glasgow weren't being brave when they didn't respond to the threats of Thomas McPherson – they just couldn't understand him. McPherson, who has a speech impediment, pointed a gun and tried to say, 'Give me the money or ...' but was unable to finish the sentence, and staff just couldn't work out what he was trying to say. One of the staff took the precaution of pressing the alarm button while McPherson stammered on, his stutter getting worse the more he tried to tell the staff what he would do if he didn't get the money. Eventually he climbed onto the counter and banged on the unbreakable screen, which was where the police found him when they arrived shortly afterwards.

UNHYGIENIC CRIM

Number one: a burglar doing a big job in a paper factory in Sweden got away with over £25,000 worth of computers. Number two: he also used the toilet, also for a big job, but omitted to flush. Police were confident that the DNA they were able to obtain from his excrement would lead to a swift arrest.

CUTE CRIM

In Ohio, Farrah Daly, 27, was arrested for stealing jewellery from her employers, Sterling Jewellers, and using the money to buy boats, horses and breast implants. At her trial she made a very strange statement, telling the judge that she was 'too cute to go to prison'. She got three years.

GIVING THEM MORE THAN THEY BARGAINED FOR

Criminals don't always get away with their crimes – sometimes their victims fight back in an astounding variety of ways. Some fight back, some bite back and some even smother them with kindness ...

When a man broke into their Florida home wielding a sawn-off shotgun, Cathy Ord, 60, and Rose Bucher, 63, did the unorthodox: instead of shrieking in terror, they offered him a ham sandwich. And a bottle of rum. And the use of their shower to freshen up and get a shave. Alfred Sweet, 52, was powerless to resist their hospitality-driven burglar prevention technique, and eventually the rum took its effect. Sweet lapsed into a drunken stupor, then passed out. A swift call to the police and the two women's five-hour ordeal was over.

A flasher in Croatia got more attention to his manhood than he anticipated. He was seen walking down a street in the city of Zagreb somewhat under the influence of alcohol. He started shouting at a woman in front of her house, then opened his trousers, got out his penis and pushed it through her fence. How was he to know that her dog was just on the other side? The dog snapped at the intruding organ and gave it a good bite. Good boy!

A 31-year-old Japanese man attacked a woman in a car park and sexually assaulted her. The victim fought back far harder than the man expected, and fastened her teeth on his right middle finger with such force that she bit it off. The man fled, but forensic scientists were able to identify him from his finger.

PRISON LIFE

In Ontario, Canada, prison inmate Joseph Hill used a hacksaw to cut a padlock on a window, enabling him to climb up onto a roof and get over the perimeter wall to freedom. Before he broke out, in a moment of foresightedness, he hid the hacksaw. His foresight proved correct – it was a matter of days before he was caught at a friend's house and thrown back inside the slammer. This time he used the hacksaw to cut through bars on a security window and then to saw another steel bar

Uganda's prison service admitted that 15 prisoners escaped near the capital, Kampala, after having weakened the jail's walls and cell bars by months of urinating on them.

before jumping to the ground from the top of a security fence. The impact broke both Hill's ankles, but he made it as far as a nearby church, where police found him in agony shortly afterwards.

In Tacoma, USA, a prisoner facing a life sentence escaped from a courtroom during the brief time his

get out of jail free

Twenty-three inmates at a prison in Mexico were handed a huge slice of freedom pie when a work-  man just happened to leave a ladder rest- ing against a perimeter wall. A worker from an electrical company was doing maintenance work at the Mazatlan prison, and, according to the prison spokesman, was not used to their secu- rity practices. One of the fleeing prisoners didn't quite make a clean getaway – he fell off the ladder and was injured. 'You have to see the funny side of it,' said the spokesman.

handcuffs and shackles were removed – using a gun made out of nothing more than paper and cardboard. He used the fake gun to threaten guards, then ditched his prison uniform and hijacked a pick-up truck to make his getaway.

Two prisoners in the UK broke out of their low- security jail on a Sunday night, and were discovered knocking on the doors of a more secure prison 20 miles away, begging to be let in. Audie Carr, 29, and Benjamin Clarke, 23, had spent the first parts of their sentences for burglary, theft and assault at Gloucester prison, where they had both managed to kick their drugs habits. Transferred to an open prison, where lax security meant plenty of drugs, they were scared that they would give in to temptation and get hooked again, so they opted for the better discipline of their old lock-up.

PRISONERS ON THE RUN

An American fugitive spent 20 years on the run after being convicted of killing his wife, then gave himself up because he couldn't repair his car. Renaldo Patterson had lived in several states since 1982 when he went on the run during his trial for the murder of his wife. Twenty years of hiding from the police, changing his name and finding places to live was wearing him down, but the

set a thief to catch a thief

A prison in Mexico was so short-staffed that it hired 42 inmates to work as prison guards. The convict-screws were paid between £20 and £100 a month to watch over prisoners at the over-crowded Tepic prison. And to make sure they had a chance of enforcing their authority, the prison bosses picked out the 42 toughest, mean-est, most terrifying jailbirds – the ones the inmates were most afraid of.

ODD

last straw was when his car broke down and his efforts to repair it didn't work. Patterson called the police and told them that it was a very long story, but he wanted to surrender. A police car was sent to collect him and his adventure was over.

THE LAW

Now even though the town of Geuda Springs, Kansas, is fairly small – a total of about 50 homes and a single paved road running through it – it has a new law that caused a big splash when it was passed by the city council. This law requires every 'head of household' to own a gun – and ammunition. Apparently, the motivation behind the law, presented and passed in one meeting, was to show neighbouring communities that the townspeople of Geuda Springs weren't afraid to carry guns. And all this in a town that has no police department and hence no one to enforce the law.

Here's a bit of a legal paradox from the US state of Kentucky: a man shot and killed by a policeman, who was charged with his murder, was charged with drugs and weapons offences. Michael Newby was shot in an incident outside a liquor store in the city of Louisville, by policeman McKenzie Mattingly. Newby was apparently dealing drugs and also carrying a gun when he was shot, for which crime he was posthumously charged – to fulfil regulations, or to prove that the good cop shot a bad criminal? Mattingly pleaded not guilty to Newby's murder.

At a New Year's Eve party in Edmonton, Canada, a man stabbed another to death, just before midnight. Because the murder took place a few minutes before 1 January, which happened to be the murderer's 18th birthday, he was transferred to the Youth Court and cannot be tried or sentenced for murder as an adult.

In a Miami courtroom, Raymond Jessi Snyder stood while his defence lawyer protested against his being jailed during the trial because he was supposedly a 'flight risk'. As his lawyer emphasised that there was no risk, Snyder sneaked from his seat and sprinted away.

THE PETTY ARM OF THE LAW

A very great masterpiece of police pettiness came to our attention last year; it was carried out in Norway. Nineteen-year-old Oysten Haakanes was sitting in the passenger seat of a friend's car at a petrol station. They had stopped there on their way home from a party, and the friend was outside the car getting some food, and had taken the car keys with him. Oysten leaned over to change a CD and nudged the gear lever into neutral, allowing the car to roll forward about three yards, before he pulled on the handbrake. Now, it so happened that a police officer has observed all this; and even though Oysten was in the passenger seat, and even though the car was not on the road, and even though the key was not in the ignition, the police officer arrested Oysten for drink-driving and achieved a conviction too.

In two separate incidents, police in Tokyo hauled in men who had used electricity without paying for it. In both instances, paying would have been a problem, even if the men had intended to, since the value of electricity used was estimated at less than half a penny. One man was caught unplugging a neon sign and recharging his mobile phone from the socket; the other was found to have unplugged a vending machine and plugged in his portable stereo to do a street perform-ance. Both men owned up to the crimes, and both received reprimands.

In Britain's National Health Service petty rule enforcement reached its zenith in this case. Dr Terence Hope, one of Britain's leading brain surgeons, was suspended from his job in the Queen's Medical Centre, Nottingham, after a dispute over how many croutons he took with his soup at lunchtime. Three patients awaiting surgery had their operations postponed

Beware of Dutch supermarkets if you are in a hurry and only want one item – you could end up behind bars. Carst Kijlstra nipped into his local Eddah supermarket in the town of Assen to get some veal to cook for his dinner. He didn't take a shopping basket because he didn't need one, and because it was almost closing time, but at the meat counter the assistant refused to serve him because he didn't have one. Mr Kijlstra's response was to put the money for the veal on the counter, and take it home. The supermarket owner's incredibly petty response was to call the police. A short time later, as Mr Kijlstra was cooking his dinner, the police turned up at his door, took him to the police station and put him in a cell, where he was kept for half an hour while they decided what to do with him, eventually fining him £95 and banning him from that supermarket for one year.

immediately, as Dr Hope, 57, was sent home after being accused of taking more croutons than a single serving, but only paying for a single serving. A very good reason for brain-injured patients to be denied the surgical skills of Dr Hope. He was eventually reinstated – even the NHS couldn't sack him for crouton-stealing – but not before those important operations were cancelled.

The city of Biloxi, in the US state of Mississippi, brought the law down on that dreadful riot-inciting activity – poetry. The Blue Bean Bistro, a restaurant in the city, had a poetry-reading night each Thursday, but city law enforcers banned it after locals complained. Maybe they didn't like the rhyming scheme, or the images were too obscure.

pettiness used against the law

The UK government announced it was to repeal an obscure law after PC Dougie Brown, on duty in the village of Nettlesham, near Lincoln, wandered into his local Co-op for a sausage roll and was refused service by shop staff. The law prohibits the sale of 'any liquor or refreshment' to an on-duty policeman without the permission of a senior officer, so staff were acting correctly, to the letter of the law, and probably with massive smugness.

UNUSUAL

Punctilious traffic police in southern Germany pulled over a driver and fined him because his dog, travelling in the back seat of the car, was not wearing a seat belt. A police spokesman defended the fine, pointing out that: 'Anything that flies forward when you brake sharply can cause serious injury and needs to be fixed securely in accordance with road safety regulations. Small dogs belong on the floor and larger dogs need to be kept in a harness or in the boot.' The driver refused to pay the fine.

Based on the premise that good communication and efficient classroom management are impossible with a minor foot problem, a Chilean teacher was told she could not take up a teaching job because she had a bunion. Nora Toro Rebeco, 47, was offered a teaching post in the town of San Bernardo, but her medical tests showed that she was unfit to teach because of a bunion on her big toe. Mrs Rebeco was appealing against the decision at the time of writing, so we can't say whether she got her foot in the door or not.

facial hair deterrent

Maybe the British bobby on the beat could learn a thing or two from this story. Police officers in Jhabua in central India were offered the equivalent of 35p extra a month to grow a moustache so they could use their whiskers as an effective tool of non-verbal communication with the public. At the time of writing seven policemen had grown moustaches to qualify for the 35p bonus. Superintendent Mayank Jain said, 'Private research showed that constables, head constables, and even sub-inspectors with moustaches were taken more seriously by the public. It added to their overall look of authority.' He went on to point out that it wouldn't do to grow any old moustache – the shape of the moustache would be monitored to prevent it from taking on a mean or vulgar twist.

WEIRD

DETERRENTS

The ultimate deterrent: the Middle Ages or a bleak vision of the future? China's Yunnan province upped the death penalty ante when it launched a fleet of 18 'mobile execution vehicles'. They are to travel the countryside so that as soon as a guilty verdict is delivered in a capital case, the lethal injection can be given straight away. Chilling.

LAWSUITS AND COURT CASES

We like this story because of the attitude of the person being sued, a traffic warden who was completely true to the stereotype. The traffic warden, a woman named only as L. Hinkson, gave a parking ticket to a motorist in Brooklyn, in New York City. The 61-year-old man was waiting in the illegally parked car while his wife was shopping, and as the warden slapped a ticket on the car, the man, Onofrio Avvinti, complained he wasn't feeling well. Having heard this sob-story most likely a thousand times before, she walked away, saying to passers-by: 'Just tell him to pay his ticket.' Little did she know that Mr Avvinti would be dead in less than ten minutes of a fatal heart attack, and that the dead man's family would sue her for $100 million, claiming that if she had radioed for help immediately, he would have been saved. A police source backed up the traffic warden, saying: 'This was a cranky old man with major health problems. I think the message is, if you have a bad heart, park legally.'

A Bulgarian woman launched a lawsuit against a heating company, claiming that they were responsible for her not conceiving another child. The 28-year-old woman said that she and her husband were trying for another baby, but that their flat had been too cold for them to have sex. The heating company in the town of Shoumen had indeed stopped supplying heat to their apartment block, because several residents had defaulted on their bills.

A court heard a wife's attempt to get her husband off a conviction of indecent exposure. In the case, in Iowa, Doug Neece was charged with exposing himself, while in a state of arousal, to a postwoman 35 ft away. Neece's wife testified that since her husband had a very small penis, you'd have to be a lot closer than 35 ft to see his erection. Her plea didn't work, and he was convicted.

And talking of genitalia, an English drug smuggler brought his into a court case and saved himself from a jail sentence. Jonathan Featherstone was caught trying to leave Jamaica with just under 16 kg of marijuana. At his trial, he claimed to be a hermaphrodite –

someone who displays both male and female charac-teristics – a fact which put Judge Valerie Stephens firmly on the back foot, since the Jamaican penal system has no arrangements for housing hermaphrodites. Featherstone's passport describes him as male, but his lawyer pointed out that he was also a 'legal and func-tional female who can get pregnant', something which would have been of interest to his fellow convicts had he been locked away in an all-male prison. Featherstone ended up with a hefty fine and walked free.

RUBBISH COPS

A policeman in Essex accidentally switched on the LED sign on the top of his patrol car that read 'POLICE, FOLLOW ME'. The police inspector, who was not named, soon had a little convoy of five law-abiding drivers following his every move as he drove around. Eventually the inspector noticed the unusual proces-sion and pulled over, but not before the group had caused traffic chaos in the town of Great Totham. The sheepish policeman was forced to apologise to the drivers, and returned to the police station to suffer the endless ribbing of his colleagues.

It's a good job that policemen Gangaran Rane and his partner S.A. Khandang weren't employed on a quota basis, because they would have been out on their ears long, long ago. To say that they were having a barren period would be understating the case. In his 36 years of police service in Mumbai, Rane had not made a single arrest. And in his 28 years Khandang had notched up one solitary success, when he caught some house-breakers, back in 1991. Last year though was their great breakthrough: they succeeded in arresting four armed robbers. True to their useless nature, they didn't do too much of the spadework themselves. Out on patrol, they were alerted by local residents that the robbers were at work in a nearby tenement; and when the pair arrived at the scene of the crime they found that residents had already overpowered the robbers. All that remained was for them to escort the robbers to the police station and then take the credit for the arrest.

American Thomas Martin McGouey, 51, of Tennessee, made a damn fine effort to get himself shot to death. Seemingly wanting to commit suicide, he painted a bull's-eye on his body before arranging a standoff in which he pointed a gun at police officers so they would shoot him in self-defence. He reckoned without the stunning inep-titude of the Knox County sheriff's deputies, who fired 28 shots at him, missed with 27 and only grazed his shoulder with the other.

Here's a story that emerged last year after a long bout of legal tussles. Seven policemen in Egypt were stupid enough to let a man who was due to appear in court on drugs charges escape the day before his trial. They were even stupider when they tried to cover for themselves by persuading a colleague to pose as the suspect at the trial. Another defendant, who knew the wanted man, rumbled the impostor, and the seven police officers were found out. They were eventually each jailed for six months.

INSENSITIVE COPS

Cruelly ignoring both standard procedure and common courtesy, the Omaha Police Department informed Judie Howell that her son had been killed in a traffic accident by leaving a message on her telephone answering machine. The message also mentioned that the body had been taken to a funeral home. The rules say that such a grave piece of information must be delivered by a uniformed officer in person, so of course Lt Tim Cavanaugh, commander of the Internal Affairs Unit, tried to seek atonement for this gross oversight ... by sending a letter of apology.

And in south-east London three plain clothes cops arrested an innocent man (who resembled a suspect), handcuffed him and bundled him into the back of their car. But before they drove him to the copshop, they told him he would have to wait a while. The policemen phoned in to a radio game called 'Have I Got Booze For You?' in order to win some lager. The arrested man, Danny Gardiner, who had just nipped out to buy a newspaper when he was whisked away, started protesting, and the radio DJ, not knowing the situation, jokingly asked the caller to 'give him a slap' to shut him up – the other policemen willingly obliged. They eventually won four crates of lager, and finally were able to drive Danny to their police station, where their idiotic mistakes (and loutish behaviour) were revealed.

DISTURBING COPS

In Southern California a lawsuit was brought against a police sergeant, Gary Ryno, by four women who worked under him in the El Cajon Police Department. The lawsuit stated that Sgt Ryno asked the women to castrate him so that he could better serve women; that he offered to strip naked and jump into a pool at an employee get-together; and that his very visible wearing of women's underwear at work was rather distressing. Just a normal Californian police officer, then.

A French policeman was stopped at the wheel of his car after a car chase involving fellow officers through the suburbs of Paris. When he was finally stopped, he was found to be drunk, and wearing nothing more than a pair of fishnet tights. So not quite standard issue uniform, then. The rogue police officer admitted he was a part-time prostitute, and that he needed the extra income.

CONCESSIONS FOR COPS

Because police work is so stressful that it affects their relationships, hundreds of Danish policemen were given free lessons on how to improve their sex lives by the Danish police federation, who hired sexologists for the task. Five hundred policemen in southern Jutland were given the chance to get free sex advice, in order to produce a happier, more satisfied and hence more effective police force.

A German policeman took his demand for a special concession to court, where it was summarily rejected. Believe it or not, his complaint was that when taking his exams to become a chief inspector, he should not be made to write on lined paper. He had always taken his tests on unlined paper, he said, and having to follow those pesky lines would require so much concentration that he would not be able to focus on the actual questions he was answering. And believe it or not, he lost his case.

EAGLE-EYED COP

A woman in West Virginia was seen by millions of viewers on live TV as she was rescued from her car during terrible flooding. Christy Walker was surrounded by 6 ft of water and was crying for help as volunteer firefighters managed to pull her clear of danger, with news cameras filming every heartwarming minute. One viewer who remained unmoved by these scenes was Deputy Sheriff David Bailey, who recognised a driver he had arrested a few months earlier. Knowing that Walker had been banned from driving at the time of the flood rescue, Bailey had Walker arrested again, and she pleaded guilty in court to driving on a revoked licence.

Pillars of the Community

Power corrupts in weird ways ...

PRIESTS

A Catholic priest in New Mexico, USA, vented his anger against a dead man in an extraordinary way. To quote the words that the unhinged Rev. Scott Mansfield was heard to say at the funeral of Ben Martinez, 'The Lord vomited people like Ben out of his mouth to Hell.' The Reverend Mansfield was angry that Martinez had not attended church during the last year of his life; the Martinez family were, predictably, suing for distress and humiliation.

'Please God, help me cleanse the computer of viruses and evil photographs which disturb and ruin my work ... so that I shall be able to cleanse myself (of sin).' This is the prayer dreamed up by Rabbi Shlomo Eliahu, to help Jews deal with the guilt of surfing pornographic websites. He came up with the prayer after noting a huge increase in the number of men coming to him to confess their sinfully smutty Internet behaviour, and recommended that they recite the prayer as they log on.

Some priests cut themselves some slack in their daily life ... A Roman Catholic priest in the US state of Ohio was arrested for growing marijuana in his church living quarters. The Reverend Richard Arko, 40, was charged with illegal cultivation of marijuana after police found a marijuana growing system in a spare bedroom and confiscated about 35 potted marijuana plants, along with grow lights, electric transformers, air purifiers and instruction books for growing marijuana.

And some priests are stricter than strict ... Father Salvatore Traina, a Catholic priest in Agrigento, in Sicily, refused to bless a health food shop because some of the products it sold were supposed to have aphrodisiac effects. It is the custom for new shops to be blessed when they are first opened, and the owner, Alessio Sansone, was a little indignant about the refusal. But the shop stocked incense and pills claimed to increase sex drive, and Father Traina was adamant that if he so much as set foot in the shop it would be against the Church's teachings, and sanctioning products that claimed to increase sexual activity ... well, that was totally out of the question.

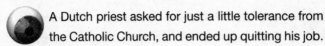

A Dutch priest asked for just a little tolerance from the Catholic Church, and ended up quitting his job. Father Stefan van Dierendonck, of Nijmegen, found out that he was allergic to wheat gluten, after years of feeling sick every time he ate the wafers used in Holy Communion. In his early career, he had to celebrate three masses a day, which made him so ill he would spend the rest of the day in bed or on the toilet. The Catholic Church allowed him to use low-gluten wafers, which were no better, but refused him the possibility of using gluten-free wafers. After the Vatican advised him to see a psychiatrist, Father Stefan decided his health was more important than his faith (bashing your head against a brick wall isn't good for your health), and left the Church.

There was a guest preacher at the First Baptist Church in Hardin County, Ohio, and he was taking repentance as his theme. Seconds after demanding that God provide him with a sign, a thunderbolt hit the church steeple, blowing out the sound system and enveloping the preacher (who was unhurt). The church was set on fire and damage was estimated at $20,000. Must have been a fair few sinners in that congregation. And who was that preacher?

QUIRKY

A nun? Drunk? A drunk nun driving? A drunk nun driving a tractor? Yep, all those things happened outside the convent in the Polish town of Krzeszow, where the 45-year-old servant of God drove the tractor into a parked car, and, when police came, was too drunk to blow into the breathalyser bag. Way to go, sister!

POLITICIANS

Politicians tend to be vain, but it is rare that their vanity stands them in good stead. In the case of Brazilian politician Jose Genoino, though, it saved him from being kidnapped. Genoino was leaving his apartment in Sao Paulo to appear on a TV show when he suddenly realised that he had forgotten something

The Mayor of Ecuador's biggest city took a highly unusual tack in an effort to ward off 'undesirable' political questions. Jaime Nebot, Mayor of Guayaquil, hired a parrot to speak on his behalf and presented it to journalists at a press conference. The parrot's function, said the Mayor, was to deal with the 'nonsense talk' that he gets from the press and that prevents him from devoting important time to his work.

absolutely vital – his comb. Leaving his press assistant and driver in the car, he hurried back inside, returning to find that they had disappeared: they had been kidnapped and robbed seconds after he had gone back for his comb.

Why is it that certain people in certain positions feel that they are above the law? Why are they usually politicians? Two French ministers, one the minister for transport, the other in charge of law and order, were caught speeding on their way to a ceremony in a Paris suburb. The predictable irony is that the ceremony was to unveil the country's first automatic radar speed traps. On a road with a speed limit of 70 kmph (42 mph) they were clocked at 100 kmph (62 mph) and 104 kmph (64 mph) respectively.

Politicians represent the public, so they ought to be ready at all times to deal with matters of public interest. Not Bengie Regensberg of the US state of New Mexico's House of Representatives. Called upon to vote on a debate on health insurance taxes, he was eventually located by state police in a motel, naked, very aggressive and somewhat the worse for drink. He had to be handcuffed and taken away to perform his duty.

LAWYERS AND JUDGES

It's hard to love distant figures of authority like judges – which could be why a judge in France had to resort to a seedy little act of self-love. But why he did it in public is anyone's guess. Three witnesses in a court in Angoulême, including a lawyer and a journalist, reported seeing the unnamed magistrate raise his gown, open his trousers and perform 'unmistakable movements', while an attorney was pleading his case.

A German lawyer turned up at a Berlin court to defend a client, and had the tables turned on him suddenly. The judge who was trying the case had the presence of mind to realise that the court documents didn't have the address of the lawyer's firm, so he did a quick check and found that the lawyer was wanted for not paying a fine for tax fraud. Just two minutes after sitting down to defend his client, the lawyer was sentenced to 15 days in jail.

A Finnish judge – who often ruled in drink-driving cases – was charged with being drunk in charge of a court. The judge, a woman in her late 50s, was trying a criminal case when lawyers stated that they believed she was drunk. An alcohol test showed her blood-alcohol level was more than three times over Finland's legal limit for driving.

When a hairdresser says, 'Oooh, love, who on earth cut your hair?' and you gleefully tell them that they did, it's all fairly harmless. But when it's the law, it's a little more serious. A judge in Australia, Justice Dean Mildren, was trying the case of an apparently incorrigible career criminal, a serial burglar by the name of Tristan Ellis, who had been granted bail the last time he had been before a court, on 28 separate charges, and had immediately gone out burgling. 'Who is the idiot,' he asked, 'who did that?' Mildren was suitably embarrassed when he was informed that it was him.

TEACHERS

Teaching ethics aren't what they used to be. At least not in Michigan, USA, where an assistant school principal tried to get a student expelled by planting drugs in his locker. Pat Conroy admitted putting marijuana in the boy's locker at Haven High School because he suspected him of being a drug dealer. His dastardly plan failed because a sniffer dog failed to find the drugs planted in the locker during a school search, but police did find marijuana in his desk.

A Belgian headmaster ended up getting the sack after attempts to toughen up his 11- and 12-year-old pupils went a bit too far. On a summer camp he forced girls with long hair to have it cut short, and he made them all watch horror films, forbidding them to look away from the screen when they were frightened. Koen Deca said he wanted them to 'cross their own borders, which cannot happen without pain or passion'.

Cheating. It's despicable. And the head teacher of a school who catches a student cheating in an exam should come down like a ton of bricks. Harnek Singh, head teacher of a school in northern India, went even further. He opened fire on a 20-year-old student Sandip Singh for smuggling notes during exams and killed him, apparently after warning him to stop.

and a dentist

According to testimony at a disciplinary hearing, a dentist from London held a patient hostage for unpaid fees by drilling a hole in her tooth then threatening not to fill it unless he got his money immediately. The patient owed Neville Kan about £60, and in her testimony said that she wanted to run away, but with her gold crown drilled to the root was in too much pain to do so. 'Nothing in life is free,' he is alleged to have cackled, as he wielded his whining, screaming drill.

Sport

The world of sport is often a conservative, fairly serious one, despite the fact that sport is supposed to be fun. There are people who remember how it ought to be though and they inject just enough weirdness to keep us going.

Last year saw that rarity, the invention of a new sport: chess boxing. This supreme test of brain and body is run by the WCBO (World Chess Boxing Organisation), and the inaugural bout took place in Amsterdam between a German artist and a Dutch lawyer, both weighing in at 75 kg. After months of hard training in the gym and at the chessboard Iepe the Joker took on Luis the Lawyer in an 11-round world championship contest, with the rounds alternating between four minutes of chess and two minutes of boxing. Iepe the Joker won in the final round when Luis the Lawyer ran out of time on his chess clock.

The Running of the Bulls in Pamplona: mean, mad-eyed, muscled beasts, their ebony-black bodies glistening, horns ready to gore the unwary, thundering along the ancient, narrow city streets as agile, daring young men leap out of their way at the very last second, as they have done for generations. And now, in the small New Zealand town of Te Kuiti: the Running of the Sheep. 2,000 woolly sheep were run through the town centre, and the biggest danger was that the sheep might trot off and get lost. Instead of the spectators jumping out of the way of the animals, the animals got out of the way of the spectators, who were often required to help keep the dim-witted creatures on the right route.

Underground running is a bit of a growth sport these days, what with races in a Swedish mine, and a marathon held in London's Greenwich Foot Tunnel under the River Thames. Last year saw the first cave marathon, held in Holland's Valkenburg Caverns, with over 100 competitors running 25 laps of slightly over one mile. Belgian Marc Papanikitas won in 2 hours 40 minutes.

Celebrating God in an uplifting way, a Bosnian priest was unofficially crowned the world's strongest clergyman after lifting a 20-stone set of weights. Father Ante Ledic, 38, broke the Bosnian weightlifting record in front of parishioners in the town of Kostajnica. Ledic took up weightlifting to keep fit, trains for over two hours a day and confirmed that his priestly sporting practice in no way interfered with his spiritual practice.

In an amateur football match in Chile, things were at fever pitch. Bandera de Chile scored against La Gonzalina in the very last minute of a game that the referee had already had to stop as rival fans brawled on the pitch. After the restart, Bandera's ace striker, El Rulo, put the ball into the net for the winning goal – and one of the La Gonzalina players immediately pulled a gun out of his shorts and fired three times at the scorer as he celebrated his goal, with one of the bullets hitting El Rulo in the shoulder.

In Europe, football managers tend to resign when the club can't afford to pay them. In Colombia, a coach resigned because his players couldn't afford to eat. Diego Umana, coach of first division club Quindio, arrived at training one day to find that four of his first-team players had not eaten at all on Monday and who had not had breakfast on Tuesday. The owners of their accommodation were not allowing them food because the rent had not been paid by the cash-strapped club.

Surfing is a sport that has its spiritual, maybe even loopy side. Back in 1976, on Leap Day – 29

February – Dale Webster, of California, USA, made a solemn vow that he would surf every day until Leap Day fell again on the fifth Sunday of February. That meant 10,407 consecutive days on his board, riding the waves – 28 whole years of daily surfing until 29 February 2004. In order to complete his task, Webster put off marriage for ten years while his girlfriend, Kaye, now his wife, recorded the daily surfing for posterity. He took low-paying night jobs so his mornings would be free, and he never went on holiday. He even surfed on his wedding day and the day his daughter was born. Now he needs ear surgery to remove calcium deposits built up by the relentless exposure to water, and his eyes are partially covered with scar tissue from 28 years of looking into the sun.

A group of swimmers embarked upon a pretty weird odyssey – to swim across Australia on the back of a truck. The pool was specially built for the purpose, and the truck was to adhere to a rigid 90 kph (55 mph) speed limit to avoid spillage. The core of ten swimmers, to be augmented by celebrities and guest swimmers along the way, set off from Geraldton in Western Australia, aiming for Sydney, about 6,000 km and 18 days away, and swam tethered in the 7.5 m pool, swimming in place while the truck motored along.

WEIRD

Following on from last year's report of a rugby league player with a tooth embedded in his arm, we can now inform you that the toughness stakes in that toughest of sports have been well and truly raised. After a UK rugby league match between Widnes Vikings and Castleford Tigers, Vikings' Aussie hooker Shaner Millard was treated for a head wound. Millard had badly gashed his bonce when he collided with a Castleford man, Dean Ripley, but he was given a temporary patch-up at half-time and returned gamely to the battle, as indeed did Ripley. As the Widnes club doctor took a little more time to treat Millard after the match, he found that there was a tooth embedded in his head. And it turned out that Ripley had finished the match with half a tooth missing.

There are many sports in which blind people participate at championship level, and one of them is golf; and the World Champion is Englishman David Morris, whose unsighted golfing skill has won him two world titles. However, just as this edition went to press it transpired that Mr Morris's wonderful ability to hit a golf ball into the middle of the fairway from verbal instructions only may be based on the fact that he can see. The English Blind Golf Association were in possession of a video that was supposed to show Mr Morris walking briskly and confidently around his home town of Newquay without a stick, swerving to avoid a dog.

And an acquaintance, a council official, claimed that Mr Morris waved at him in the street, then lowered his hand quickly when he realised what he had done.

FITNESS

News reached us last year of a British supermarket testing a prototype of a very unusual shopping trolley. Tesco's Trim Trolley is a mobile piece of gym equipment that lets you fill it up and get fit while you're doing it (then go home and fill your face with food again). The trolley has an adjustable resistance wheel that lets you use more or less effort to push the trolley around the store, while it monitors heart rate, calories burnt, length of workout and speed of the trolley.

fatness

Jack Taylor of Bradford had not left his house for 25 years because he feared comments about his size. No wonder; he weighs 50 stone (700 lb, or 318 kg). However, when he fell over at home and broke his leg last year he had to call the emergency services. It took a team of no fewer than ten fire-fighters to manoeuvre him onto a stretcher.

Food & Drink

As long as people keep wanting to feed their faces, the stories will keep rolling in.

MMMM, PIZZA!

Pizza can be addictive (so a friend tells me!), so if you need more pizza in your life you can enjoy it in your bathwater, wash in it and rub it on your body after washing (which definitely involves fewer calories). This is because Ducio Cresci, a cosmetics producer from Florence, has created a range of products that smell of pizza. Aiming for a pizza experience that indulges more than just the stomach, Cresci has produced a bubble bath, soap and body lotion that contain extracts of tomato, basil and oregano, leaving your skin with a faint tang of pizza. And if you want the whole meal experience in your bathroom, there is also Tuscan bread body lotion, cappuccino soap and oils scented with chocolate and cake.

 Last year UK supermarket Sainsbury's trialled a weird and wonderful new breed of tomato. The

Kumato tomato is black, and is the result of six years of research. The story goes that it was noticed that the black tomato, which originates from the Galapagos Islands, enhanced the sex lives of the famous Galapagos giant tortoises, giving strength to the old idea that tomatoes are an aphrodisiac.

Christmas comes around every year, and always a lot sooner than we expect. And every year, a lot sooner than his colleagues expect, supermarket food-tester Tony Vaughan, who works for Tesco, starts on his seasonal testing diet of five kilograms of Brussels sprouts a week. He does his eating and tasting in the food-testing kitchens, but when he returns to his desk to deal with suppliers, his colleagues kick up a stink. Tony, surrounded by a haze of sprouty gas, is obliged to sit near a window. They have even hung a warning sign over his desk, although as yet they have not resorted to gas masks.

Here's a story from Scotland that would make any gourmet, bon viveur or foodie shudder in horror. A London journalist (hence the story hitting the public domain) and his girlfriend were staying in the Aviemore ski resort in the Scottish Highlands. She ordered a bowl of chilli con carne and was given a bowl of mince. She asked for some sour cream, and the waiter produced an aerosol can of fake cream and sprayed it over the mince. And when she complained that it was not actually sour cream, he got a Jif plastic lemon and squirted some juice over the cream.

And another example of a gourmet gastronomical experience combining quality service and delicious food, this time from New Zealand. Johannus Roes had ordered a burger in Brucie's Diner, in Auckland, but

How many layers of weirdness can you cope with? A sado-masochistic restaurant? In Israel? With really good food, so in theory there's nothing to complain about? Israel's first (and only, and maybe last) sado-masochist restaurant, The Dungeon, opened its doors in the old southern Tel Aviv suburb of Yaffo. Diners were welcomed by a hostess squeezed into a black vinyl outfit, brandishing a whip, while the serving staff, male and female, were also severely yet skimpily clad. The restaurant is not BYOS – Bring Your Own Shackles – as shackles are thoughtfully provided for diners to tie themselves to their table. Any complaints about the food, served from a French bistro-style menu, are met with a whipping or being suspended in an iron cage from the ceiling, but owner Amos Levy stressed his desire to provide excellent food 'in an alternative framework'.

STRANGE

complained that the chef who made it had dirty hands, was not wearing gloves, and had wiped his forehead while preparing it. The cook's response was to hurl the dirty burger at Roes, but he missed. The filthy burger was so dense that it smashed a window.

While Scotland rejoices in its deep-fried Mars bars and Kit Kats, a sweets company in the Ukraine brought out a real challenge in the form of one of the unhealthiest snacks you could possibly stuff into your face – pure pork fat covered in chocolate. Its name translates as 'Fat in Chocolate', and the finger-sized treat of artery-clogging madness is no more nor less than a stick of dark chocolate with a rich seam of white lard inside. Bet you can't eat three.

Talking about Mars bars ... a Lebanese woman walked into a branch of Woolworth's in London and took advantage of their 'five bars for £1' offer by buying up the store's entire stock of Mars Bars. She ended up with 10,656 bars, which she got her chauffeur to load into her black stretch limo, while she liberated a wad of fresh £50 notes to meet the bill for £2,131.20. She must really have needed to work, rest and play.

Here's a drink so cool it made the drinker's tongue go numb. A man working in a warehouse in Florida noticed a damaged can of orange juice that seemed a bit off. He took a sip and immediately his tongue went numb – not surprising, since the juice, in a consignment from Jamaica, contained liquid cocaine with a street value of about $40,000.

A letter to a 'Parenting' column in the US state of Rhode Island, and its reply, came to our notice last year. The reader's problem was this: 'I can't keep my 20-month-old daughter out of the dog's food. I've tried scolding, distracting, time-out, nothing has worked.' The reply from John Rosemond, parenting expert, was: 'From a strictly nutritional standpoint, most dog food is superior to the diets of many Americans ... A paediatrician said he has yet to see a child who suffered ill effects from eating dog food, except for chunk-type that might get stuck in the throat.'

DON'T EAT THAT, YOU DON'T KNOW WHERE IT'S BEEN

Oral gratification never looked so weird ...

Deep in the rural heart of West Virginia – hillbilly country – the Pocahontas County Harvest Festival came up with a novel attraction: a cooking competition using roadkill. Alongside the bluegrass bands and truck and tractor shows, the roadkill cook-off is a big draw to the festival, and features recipes using possum, squirrel, rattlesnake and bear. Prizes are awarded based on showmanship, taste and originality. One of the festival sponsors is the Pocahontas Humane Society.

The grim result of a wacky bet caused the *Medical Journal of Australia* to issue the following warning to Australians: do not eat slugs. A student in Sydney accepted a $20 bet to eat a slug and contracted a potentially deadly form of meningitis from it. A friend who had joined in the slugfest was saved from the serious illness because he made himself throw up after his slug-swallowing adventure. The ill student's meningitis, which made his brain lining swell up, was caused by a worm carried as larva by slugs and snails, and was grave enough to keep him in hospital for 17 days and away from his studies for five months.

This eating story happened a couple of years ago, but, like many stories, came to light this year as a result of a long-drawn-out court case. Sophie Matlala, a hospital cleaner in South Africa, opted for the goulash at the canteen of the Medforum Hospital in Pretoria, and as she tucked into it, came across a lump of meat that she was unable to chew. Further inspection revealed the meat to be a piece of cooked penis. Whether the organ was human or animal, no one could establish. Ms Matlala is now a vegetarian.

A 39-year-old Thai man made the news last year when it was revealed that he had been eating a live worm a day for the last thirty years or so. Paisit Chanta, a firefighter, first ate a worm while out fishing as a boy, reasoning that if fish could eat worms without becoming ill, then so could he. Every day since then Chanta has sucked down a live worm, and credits his excellent state of health to his special dietary supplement, which he now chews carefully instead of swallowing whole.

It was very ironic: a Chinese woman gave her three children and their cousin a special dish designed to improve their digestion. But it didn't improve their digestion – it killed them. The dish was a soup made from toads, freshly captured in the wild. The skin of the toad carries a deadly poison, so although the meat is, supposedly, delicious and nutritious, you have to prepare it pretty carefully. And if you don't, no matter how bad your digestion is, it can be fatal.

Police found Jurgen Tersago, from Aalst in Belgium, crawling around a field, grunting like a pig and contentedly grazing on the grass. He'd started by crawling out of his car onto the field and he was crawling because he was drunk. In court for driving under the influence of alcohol he told the judge that he especially liked eating grass when he was drunk, and that it tasted like spinach to him.

AND DON'T DRINK THAT, EITHER ...

Staff at a petrol station in Halle, Germany first looked on in amazement, then called the police, as they witnessed a man approach one of the fuel pumps, put the nozzle to his mouth and drink. According to the police, the 30-year-old man chose unleaded, and

What you do when you feel your sex drive is on the wane? If you're out in a rural area of China, chances are you'll follow an old folk remedy. But when the remedy is rat's urine, you can bet it won't do you much good. Yang Qunying, 50, set some bait in her pigsty to trap a female rat, waited till it emptied its bladder and drank the urine to boost her kidney energy. She ended up in hospital with breathing difficulties and cyclomastopathy, or swollen breasts. Maybe that's how it really works – larger breasts, increasing the sex drive ... of men.

swallowed about a quarter of a pint. He paid for it, so it wasn't illegal – just very, very weird.

A 42-year-old Russian invited journalists to his home town of Lipetsk to watch him drink a litre of antifreeze. Dmitry Butakov apparently was of the belief that he was immortal, a state of mind induced by his having survived a massive electric shock 12 years earlier, and had a party piece that involved swallowing a ball of mercury. So down went the first half-litre of anti-freeze, and he appeared to be OK; but after the second half-litre, he collapsed, went into a coma and died.

Animals

We humans are only animals, really, so it's no wonder that we can empathise with them so much and create so much weirdness together.

How much devotion can you show towards a horse? Maybe you could turn it into a house pet? Even give it its own house? How about giving it your own house? Now that really is devotion. An Indian couple moved out of their apartment near Mumbai to make room for their new horse, Akash. Vikas Wavale and his wife Sarika, of Dombivili, bought Akash for about £600 at a market in Pandharpur, and Viukas had his wife trained by a jockey so that she could ride him each day to stop him getting muscle cramps from being in the small apartment.

And how much consideration can you give to domestic animals? Firefighters carry oxygen masks to keep people breathing as they rescue them from burning buildings. Well, last year firefighters in Florida started carrying oxygen masks for cats, dogs and even hamsters, to help save pets suffering from smoke inhalation.

Paloma Bärtschi, from Zürich, started offering lessons in how to speak to animals at the bargain price of £360 per lesson. Apparently her pet rabbit Spot was her teacher trainer, so to speak, who, said Paloma, gave her instructions on how to communicate telepathically with animals.

A Scottish farmer took highly creative action to protect her flock of sheep, after several sightings of a big cat prowling the area. Charlotte Brayley made patterned stencils and then applied red, green and purple paint on six of her animals. The stripes act as

In the last edition of *Another Weird Year* we told you about Aalfie, a German eel that had been living in a family's bath for 34 years. Well, Aalfie hit the news again last year, when he became probably the first eel ever to win an advertising contract. In exchange for appearing in commercials for a German pet food store, Aalfie was given a lifetime supply of mosquito larvae. Aalfie has lived in the Richters' bath in Bochum ever since he was caught by Paul Richter 34 years ago, and the kids refused to let their father cook him.

ODD

camouflage, making it more difficult for the predatory cat to see the shape of its prey. The sightings had been of a black, leopard-like cat, and Ms Brayley, who also attends Glasgow School of Art, did not want to allow any of her flock to fall prey to the beast.

One minute Ray Dushkin Jr was standing on the side of his grandfather's fishing boat in a dock in Alaska; the next moment a sealion leapt out of the water, grabbed him and pulled him into the sea. Sealions swimming around a fishing boat with a freshly caught haul of fish are a common occurrence, but for a sealion to jump six feet in the air and pull a man into the water is unheard of – until now. The creature let go of Dushkin after a few moments, leaving him unharmed apart from a large graze in his left buttock. What a story to tell the grandchildren.

MUTT SHADES

A German firm has started designing sunglasses for dogs. Originally they were to protect mountain rescue dogs from the harsh glare of sun on snow, but the company had so much call for their product that they've come up with a whole designer range. Prices on the British market range between £40 and £60, with protection from sun, sand and snow guaranteed. Adjustable straps keep the shades in place on different shapes and

it's a dog's life

A Japanese department store offered loving dog owners the chance to treat their precious ones to a very special New Year's meal. Playing the exclusivity card in order to cash in, the Mitsukoshi store was charging £145 for a 'bento' box containing 30 traditional Japanese dishes including pork dumplings, black beans, chicken balls, roast beef, ham and even green tea and strawberry mousse. The store already successfully sells swimsuits and kimonos for dogs.

sizes of doggie heads, even when indulging in rough-and-tumble with poochy pals, and mirror lenses are available, as well as a variety of frame colours. And a gold frame especially for Yorkshire terriers.

For dog owners who want their hounds to be in the peak of condition, a gym exclusively for dogs opened in the Chilean capital, Santiago. With personal trainers on hand to whip those pooches into shape and of course a range of treadmills for dogs to run on, the gym, opened by Ezio Solari, also has a beauty parlour and dog show preparation classes for owners.

A dog was the unwitting cause of a grass fire in the US state of Idaho during the summer, after a bizarre chain of events. The dog's owner had run out of petrol, and stopped to refill the tank. As he restarted his van, it backfired and sparks ignited petrol fumes near the dog, whose fur caught fire. The driver let the poor creature out of the car, and it immediately rolled in dry grass to put out the flames, setting the grass alight. Firefighters had to come to extinguish the blaze. The dog was reported to be unharmed.

In Berlin, a man named only as Roland T was arrested for breaking Germany's anti-Nazi laws when it was discovered that he had taught his dog, Adolf, to give the Nazi salute. Complaints from members of the public led to a police investigation, and when they quizzed the owner of Adolf (a German Shepherd cross) he demonstrated his dog's ability to mimic Hitler. Despite Germany's strict laws against the use of Nazi symbols, Roland T, who wears an Adolf Hitler-style moustache, said he didn't know what the fuss was about, and that he had been brought up to behave this way.

The owner of a Staffordshire bull terrier (they're the tough-looking ones) in Russia paid the ultimate price for having an aggressive dog. He had a heart attack, but his dog held off paramedics trying to save his life. The police were called, and they were forced to shoot the dog – but it was too late. By that time the man was dead.

A guard dog did the exact opposite of what it was supposed to do and paid the ultimate price. Sun Xiaoshan, a mason in China's Hubei province, left his dog guarding a pile of cash with a value of about £215 while he and his wife went out to work. When they returned, the dog had eaten most of the banknotes, with about £50 left. The enraged Xiaoshan promptly killed his dog and tried to retrieve the cash – surprisingly he managed to get enough out of the dog to be able to fit together 14 more banknotes.

A little doggie was found in a public park in the US state of South Carolina, apparently abandoned because he had five legs. Poor little Popcorn, a Maltese

man bites dog

The classic headline takes a further twist: in eastern China, a man was walking home with friends after a night out when a dog nipped him on the fingers and cheek, so he repeatedly bit the dog until it died.

terrier cross, was taken to an animal hospital, where he was operated on to relieve his condition. Unfortunately, he went from having one leg too many to one leg too few: not only did the fifth leg have to be removed but also the leg next to it, which had not properly developed. It truly is a dog's life.

CATS

'What's that you say, Puss-Puss? A little woolly baa-lamb? Drowning in the swimming pool?' Yes, it really happened: gardeners Adrian Bunton and Karen Lewis, working in the garden of the house of Jill Royle, in Gloucestershire, were alerted by their cat Puss-Puss that something was wrong, as she ran frantically up to them and away from the house's swimming pool, miaowing anxiously. The couple quickly followed her to the pool where they found an escaped lamb in difficulties. Thanks to their cat's action, the lamb's life was saved.

A UFO visited the town of Lardal in Norway – or that was the conclusion that local people came to after an explosion was heard and a fiery light seen drifting slowly earthward. Oslo University astrophysicists stated that it was definitely not a meteorite; the Lardal electricity company confirmed no power problems. However, they were forced to look again at their records after the charred corpse of a cat was found underneath a power mast, and a four-second dip coinciding with the time of the 'UFO' sightings showed that a daring cat must have climbed the power mast and burst into flames when its tail caught a high-voltage cable, causing a short-circuit that also set the wooden pole alight.

A kitten was sucked up into a street sweeping machine in Melbourne and trapped inside it until the operator of the machine checked the contents of the chamber to find the tiny creature barely alive. He blew into its nostrils to make its lungs start working again and took it to a local animal clinic, where the seven-week-old kitty returned to normal health after its miraculous escape. The vets, astounded that the kitten had survived such a deadly ordeal, named it 'Hoover'.

More proof of the nine lives principle came from the US state of Michigan, when Jamie Muniz saw her cat, Debo, wander into her back garden about a week after disappearing, apparently very hungry and in search of his food bowl. Her relief gave way to horror when she realised that the poor beast had two arrows sticking right through his head. After they were removed, Debo was worse off to the tune of a missing eye, but was otherwise fine.

You don't usually expect to be able to have much influence over a cat. That is one of their attractions. But Sarah Walker seems to have had the wrong sort of influence over her darling pet, Ebony. First, a few years ago, Mrs Walker, of Suffolk, fell off her motorbike and broke her right leg; one month later Ebony had to have his right leg amputated after being hit by a car. Later, she had surgery to remove a painful wisdom tooth; Ebony had all his teeth taken out a few weeks later due to gum disease. This last year, Mrs Walker had an operation on her left eye because she was suffering from double vision, just a fortnight after Ebony had to have his left eye removed after an ulcer burst. Mrs Walker is now dreading her next illness ...

A cat was born in the Samara region of Russia with three ears. Cats normally have two, so that's a bit unusual. Not nearly so unusual, though, as what happened after it was born. The kitten carried on growing ears, until it had a total of seven, adding four more extraneous ears to the single surplus it was born with. The first extra ear appeared inside one of its original ears, then two more popped up inside the other ear, then two more started growing on its cheek. The kitty was otherwise completely normal, apparently, so that means nine lives and seven ears.

CONTRACT KILLINGS

Why would criminals want to whack a poor defence-less critter?

Blaze, an English springer spaniel working in Iraq, nearly got extinguished. He works with the British armed forces in southern Iraq, making use of his skills in sniffing out guns, ammunition and explosives, and he got away with injuries when a car deliberately swerved into him and ran him over. 'There is no doubt that this was a deliberate assassination attempt,' a senior army officer was quoted as saying. 'We are convinced that there was a price on Blaze's head.' Blaze made a full recovery from his injuries.

A sniffer cat specialising in detecting caviar poach-ers met his end beneath the wheels of a poacher's car in the Stavropol region of Russia. The cat, named Rusik, had been taken in as a stray by the officers at one of the regional police stations, fed fish confiscated from poachers, and turned out to have a good nose for caviar. He was better in this respect than sniffer dogs, and since caviar poaching is a particular problem in that area, was a valuable addition to the force. The car that killed him was a car that Rusik had found caviar in some time before, and his commanding officers were of the opinion that Rusik had had a contract put out on him, and his death was a brutal gangland assassination.

FLYING BEASTS

Cows were *still* launching themselves into thin air last year, not realising that they would plummet rather than soar.

When Derrick and Patricia Cogan arrived at their caravan on its site in North Devon for a holiday, the site owner had some bad news for them. He told them that their caravan had been hit by a low-flying cow. The caravan had been stored in a disused quarry; the cow had been grazing a little too close to the edge, slipped and tumbled 30 feet onto the caravan, causing £2,000 worth of damage. The Cogans still managed to enjoy their holiday, despite the damage, and put in an insurance claim that had their insurers, Caravan Guard, in hysterics. The cow was injured, but recovered.

A Turkish woman suffered the indignity of being landed on by a flying cow that actually belonged to her. Nazmiye Serengil, from Mus, was grazing her cows on a field next to a railway track, and one of the herd

magpie mouse

Staff at Woodroffe's, a jeweller's in the Welsh town of Newtown, began to notice that odd earrings were occasionally going missing from the shop but thought nothing of it until £500 worth of gold earrings disappeared from the shop window. An exhaustive search of the shop eventually uncovered a hole in the floorboards leading to a mouse's nest lined with bubble wrap and till receipts. In the nest were the missing earrings. A pest controller was called ...

strayed onto the rails just as a train came by. The impact flung the cow several metres into the air and it landed on Serengil. She sustained nothing more than a broken foot, while the fate of the poor cow went unrecorded.

An overcurious cow fell into a three-metre deep well in the hills near Adelaide, Australia, and no matter how everyone tried they were unable to haul the beast out, even with 15 members of the Country Fire Service lending their expertise. Then someone had the bright idea of flooding the well and floating the cow to the top, where it could be pulled onto dry land.

WHEN ANIMALS ATTACK ...

A 60-year-old German man was only trying to do his darling pet a favour, but he ended up very much the worse for wear. The darling pet was a huge Rottweiler, and the man, from Karlsruhe, had decided that the brute needed its teeth cleaning. He reached into the dog's mouth, wielding a specially purchased canine toothbrush, and the next thing he knew was that he was being mauled and shaken. The man only survived by playing dead and letting his body relax completely, at which the Rottie went back to its kennel, teeth not clean – covered in blood, in fact. The man lost lots of blood but recovered in hospital.

In the South African village of Madipelesa a rogue baboon, an old male living on the fringes of a local troop, sneaked into a house and grabbed a three-month-old baby boy from his bedroom. Neo Tukane's mother watched helplessly as the baboon bounded to the top of a telegraph pole, ripped open the baby's skull and ate his brain. It all happened so fast that no one in the village had time to act. Having eaten the brain, the baboon threw the child's body to the ground and scampered off into the bush. It was eventually tracked down and shot.

Berlin resident Mark Voegel succumbed first to his pet black widow spider, then to the rest of his creepy zoo. Voegel, who kept a vast menagerie of snakes, lizards and insects, was fatally bitten by Bettina the black widow spider. Then his dead body became hearth, home and restaurant for his menagerie, as spiders took up residence in his corpse, thousands of termites nibbled away at his flesh, and snakes and lizards ripped chunks of flesh from his bones. Neighbours alerted police after the smell from Voegel's house became too revolting to be normal, and police broke in to find his corpse on the sofa and his zoo living off him.

Juan Evangelista Poot, 22, from Yucatan in Mexico, was standing outside his house one day when he was hit by a bullet. In agony, he turned round to see none other than his best friend in all the world – his dog – with his (Juan's, not the dog's) gun in his mouth. Somehow he had managed to fire the gun. Señor Poot was not badly hurt.

Pigs tend to eat anything – including their owners. In China's Laoning province a 73-year-old farmer, Mr San, was reported missing by his neighbours after not being seen for two days. Police found his pigs – large sow and eight piglets – crunching on human bones in the pigsty and concluded that he had fainted from lack of oxygen in the very hot, stuffy pigsty and fallen in. The neighbours said that the sow had been a

Beavers are developing a cunning strategy to wipe out the human race and take control of the planet. Fortunately for the human race it only works where forests and roads coincide, like in Norway. A beaver chewed through a tree by the side of the E6 highway near Oslo, and pushed the tree over, toppling it directly into the path of a bus. The driver managed to swerve, preventing a serious accident, but a passenger was injured by shattered glass, and the bus was badly damaged.

UNUSUAL

favourite of his ever since he first got her; so we think he probably wouldn't have minded that she ate him.

... AND DEFEND

A llama's love for its owner can be a powerful thing. But it can be a double-edged sword: ambulance crews called to the aid of a 72-year-old farmer were unable to help him because his herd of llamas rallied to his defence. Llama farmer Graham Bailey fell in a rabbit hole in a field on his farm in Northamptonshire, and was stranded for two hours before a passer-by heard his cries for help. The passer-by phoned paramedics, whose arrival in the field upset the llamas, especially

... and trap

In Australia, a man was trapped by a turkey. He was walking along a trail in the Burleigh Heads National Park on Queensland when he fell into a mating hole dug by a brush turkey. Then, in the next part of the mating ritual, the turkey is believed to have partially buried the man. He was stuck there for quite some time before the next walker alerted the rangers and they came to pull him out, fighting back the laughter.

the alpha male llama, Milo. He led his herd to form a protective ring round Bailey to stop the ambulance crew getting any closer. The llama–ambulanceman standoff was brought to an end when an air ambulance was called, and the helicopter scared the llamas away. Bailey was rescued, and treated for a fractured hip.

... AND EVEN EXPLODE

A huge sperm whale was found beached on the coast of the island of Taiwan. The massive 50-ton carcass was loaded onto a truck and driven through Tainan City to a research centre. Right in the middle of the city, the gases in the whale's belly built up to the point that it exploded, splattering cars and shops with blood, blubber and other gory sloppy bits.

THE BIRDS

Postmen and postwomen are often chased by dogs – it's a fact of mail delivery life. Japanese postman Mutsumi Oki, however, started a new round last year and discovered that while most mailmen have to watch out for dogs, he has to watch out for a pheasant. Every day, at the same point on his route, Oki is attacked by a male pheasant as he drives by on his bright red post-office motorbike. The bird sometimes attacks from the front at full speed, and occasionally lands on Oki's back and claws him. One theory is that the furious pheasant hates the red of the motorbike, which unfortunately is something that Oki cannot change.

And in a weird echo of that Japanese pheasant versus postie conflict, a postman in Devon was injured in the hand and leg after a series of attacks from a pheasant that lies in wait for him on his daily round in the town of Swimbridge. The bird, a cock pheasant, uses a variety of tactics to get ahead of Mr Patton's van, which, being bright red, is also thought to trigger the attacks.

A trained hawk employed to keep down the numbers of rats and pigeons in New York City's Bryant Park was grounded after a case of mistaken identity. The hawk swooped on a chihuahua that was nosing around the bushes in the park, severely gouging the little pooch's nose. The hawk's trainer said that the bird must have assumed the chihuahua was a rat.

In the German city of Dortmund a rogue crow was proving to be a threat to public safety. The grudge-bearing crow had been attacking passers-by in the city, so the police were brought in to apprehend the vicious bird. Their cunning plan: to put down bait laced with alcohol to get it drunk. The bait was cat food – apparently an irresistible delicacy for crows, and the alcohol

lazy birds given car to migrate south

Scientists at a research centre in Austria spent more than two years breeding a flock of a rare bird, the Northern Bald Ibis, then discovered that the birds were unable to make their winter journey to northern Italy on their own. The ibis had become used to being looked after and simply refused to fly south for the winter. So the birds were packed into a car and driven to their winter quarters. Attempts to show the birds the way south using hang-gliders are showing encouraging results, but until they have learned the way and got the get-up-and-go to make the long flight, the ibis will be sitting comfortably in the back seat of the Migration Taxi.

was high-potency fruit schnapps. It wasn't long before the crow was completely smashed, and the arrest was a formality.

PERILOUS PARROTS

Jan de Groodt, of Tegelen in southern Holland, adored his many parrots and ferrets. But he wasn't too hot on cleaning up after them. Over a period of several years festering masses of parrot shit built up in his house, causing the air inside to become so heavily laden with ammonia fumes that Mr de Groodt eventually died from inhaling it. He called the emergency services one morning saying he felt very unwell, and by the time the ambulance arrived, entering a house that resonated to the screeching of parrots and that stank to high heaven, he had collapsed and died. None of the ferrets or parrots appeared to be suffering from the fumes of their own excrement, and many of them immediately escaped when windows were opened to clear the air.

In the Ukrainian capital of Kiev, a retired policeman popped out of his flat for a few minutes, and returned to find the somewhat surprising sight of three men lying flat on the floor with their hands behind their heads. The men were thieves, but when they had broken into the flat they heard a voice – the policeman's parrot, in fact – say, 'Stop! I'll shoot! Get on the floor!', and they immediately obeyed. The parrot had never spoken a word before that day.

TROUBLE AND STRIFE

A woman in Klagenfurt, Austria, spotted some cables in the boot of her car that she didn't recognise, and called the police, who reckoned it was a car bomb. A specialist bomb-defusing robot was set to work, destroying the device with an extremely powerful jet of water, and it was then analysed. The truth was the device was a GPS tracking instrument, installed in his wife's car by her very jealous husband to monitor her movements.

A possessive spouse can be a pain. In Guyana, Courtney Purlette was much more than a pain – he was sent to prison for his hideous crime of jealousy: he thought his wife had been cleaning another man's shoes, so he hacked off her hands with a machete.

When Elaine Cassells went to confront her husband at the house of his mistress, she had a few glasses of wine to get her ready for action and drove the two miles to the other woman's house. Her husband, Stephen, was a policeman, though, and when she stormed into the front garden of his lover's house he had her arrested for drink-driving.

 Police in Germany had to deal with a rather amusing domestic incident in the city of Braunschweig.

A Romanian couple bumped into **ODD** each other at a seaside resort on the Black Sea. Victor Dragomirescu was supposedly working at his parents' house and his wife Lucica was supposedly at home ill in bed. It was because they were talking to each other on their mobile phones that they discovered that each one was living a lie. Victor was complaining about all the hard work he had to do, that he was covered in dust and faced a hard afternoon of fruit-picking. Lucica was saying that she felt worse than ever, was unable to eat and if wasn't for the boon of mobile phones wouldn't be able to get out of bed to talk to her beloved husband. It was at that moment, there on the beach, that they realised they were right in front of each other. The doubly duplicitous couple headed home after that, but said a divorce was the most likely outcome.

A 60-year-old woman had gone to the house of her ex-lover, and they decided to spend the night together. It wasn't long, though, before they got into a huge argument, culminating in the man throwing her out of his house. Unfortunately, their plans to spend the night together had been sufficiently advanced for the woman to have already taken out her false teeth. Standing outside her ex-lover's door, she pleaded for the return of her dentures, but he refused to give them back. Eventually she called the police and they managed, with difficulty, to persuade him to hand over her teeth. To spare any further embarrassment, they also drove her to the train station.

A Croatian man wasn't equal to his wife's sexual demands. After a hard day labouring on a building site, 26-year-old Svetin Gulisija found the prospect of a hard night in bed too much to deal with. Unable to light a fire in his own loins, he started a fire in the woods just behind their house in the hope that the house would catch light. The couple were evacuated by firefighters who came to deal with the blaze when it got out of hand, causing about £15,000 worth of damage. Gulisija was jailed for two blissfully sex-free years.

One minute you're a rich Turkish industrialist with bags of money and power aplenty, the next you're locked in the bathroom for three years without your clothes by your wife. The wife of Orhan Babatcu, 41, shut him up in the bathroom while she (a) cavorted around with other men; (b) claimed he was mentally ill; and (c) waited to inherit his fortune. Babatcu's mother eventually persuaded the police to intervene and his wife was arrested. Babatcu received psychiatric help (probably for a deep-rooted fear of bathroom fittings).

A very unusual nuptial contract was signed in China: the wife, Yin, was so sick of her husband's body odour that she made him sign an agreement to have a bath every day, instead of his maximum of one a week. According to the agreement, Luo, the husband, would be barred from living at home for one month if he breached the agreement three times.

In Norway, a man was fed up to the back teeth of always being his girl-friend's designated driver. So one day as he caught sight of a police car he stamped on the accelerator and bombed through a 50 mph zone at 85 mph. His dreams came true as he was banned from driving for a year – he even got a 14-day jail sentence just to keep him out of his girlfriend's way until she cooled down.

choices, choices

A German pop singer, Werner Boehm, got a female baboon as a pet, and they got on so well that the baboon started to go to bed with him. At this point his wife, Susanne, said, 'Either the baboon goes or I go.' Boehm chose the baboon and off went Susanne. However, an animal rights group complained to the police, the baboon was taken away, and lonely Werner asked his wife to come back, paying her the ultimate compliment that she was nicer to sleep next to than the baboon.

who wears the trousers?

A robber snatched a cash till with more than £1,300 in it from a shop assistant in the German town of Göttingen and sprinted off home with the money. He took it back home to his wife, but she nagged him and gave him such a verbal going-over about having resorted to crime to try and pay off their debts that he returned to the shop about an hour later and rather sheepishly handed the cash till, complete with money, back to the astounded shop assistant.

WEDDING BELLS

Tying the knot, getting hitched – but not in the normal way.

The head of a mental institution in southern China was arrested last year after four years of a very weird trade. Wang Chaoying had been selling female patients, at prices in the hundreds of pounds a head, to lonely bachelors in search of brides. Chaoying drugged the women so that the prospective husbands didn't twig that they were buying mental patients. He managed to sell over 20 women patients, sometimes being asked for his money back by enraged buyers, before he was found out.

Talk about long-drawn-out engagements. A Honduran man waited an amazing 50 years before marrying his girlfriend. Even more amazing is the fact that he lived to the age of 104 before he did so. The girlfriend, Concepcion Hernandes, who was a mere 15 years old when Lucio Cruz fell in love with her, was only 65 on their wedding day. We'd like to wish them a long and happy marriage ...

An unmarried man in China suffered the frustration and expense of having to buy a stream of costly gifts as several friends and relatives had weddings. In an attempt to claw back what he had spent, he staged his own wedding by hiring a prostitute to pose as his bride. He collected £400 in wedding presents, but was found out at the last minute by a suspicious guest.

UNHOLY ALLIANCES

Some people end up in the weirdest marriages ...

In France the law allows you to marry a dead person. Not any old dead person, but the person you were intending to marry, of course, as long as you can prove that the marriage was definitely on the cards, and as long as the Président himself gives it the thumbs-up. So, bizarre as it may seem, 35-year-old Christelle Demichel became a wife and a widow in the same ceremony performed at Nice City Hall when she married her boyfriend, Eric, killed in a car accident. Needless to say, Eric was not present for the ceremony.

A Chinese couple suffered the sad loss of their daughter, aged 28 – but then offered £75,000 to any man who would marry her. The man was to go through a formal wedding ceremony, be given an apartment and the money, and would have to stay faithful to his ghost bride. All because her mother dreamed that she was lonely in the spirit world without a hubby.

A young Indian man took the remarkable step of marrying his own grandmother so as to be better able to take care of her. Twenty-five-year-old Narayan Biswas married his 80-year-old grandmother in a traditional Hindu ceremony, saying that he could care for her better as her husband, and granny Premodas agreed, saying that he was a good husband because he made sure she got her meals on time.

The last edition of *Another Weird Year* brought you the story of a man suing one of his multiple personalities. Last year we heard about a gay Swedish firefighter, Bjorn Ullberg, who also suffers from a multiple personality disorder. Not only did two of his identities, Lars, a silver-tongued second-hand car dealer, and Siggy, a shy, retiring book lover, fall in love with each other, but he/they found a minister who was prepared to marry them. Ullberg's psychiatrist was not happy.

COURTING COUPLES

How not to get back with your girlfriend, part one: get shot in the groin. A man in the central Sicilian city of Piazza Armerina persuaded a friend to shoot him in the groin so that his ex-girlfriend would feel sorry for him, and then get back with him. The 27-year-old turned up at the hospital with wounds from a hunting rifle's pellets

How not to get back with your girlfriend, part two: chop your fingers off. A 21-year-old Chinese man, who had been dumped by his girlfriend, went to her house and chopped off three of his fingers. The idea was to prove how much he loved her – so from that point of view it was a success – and to win her sympathy so that she would take him back – which was a total failure. She didn't even go to visit him in hospital.

WEIRD

in his groin area; at first he said he had had a hunting accident, but later admitted the truth under police questioning. His girlfriend had left him because of his violent behaviour. And guess what? She never wants to see him again.

Everything was going according to plan. Brian Shipwash was cruising up Pilot Mountain, in North Carolina, on his Harley-Davidson motorbike, with his girlfriend, Shandra Miller, sitting on the passenger seat. In Brian's pocket was something special, for later. Then, on a tight bend on the winding mountain road, he lost control of the massive machine and crashed into a pick-up truck. Stretched out on the road, with six inches of Harley handlebar sticking into his abdomen, not knowing whether he would live or die, Brian desperately tried to salvage the situation. He reached into his pocket for that special item and pulled out a battered and blood-stained box with an engagement ring inside, and asked Shandra to marry him. She said yes. And his injuries weren't as bad as first feared.

German politics involves proportional representation, and one German man carried the idea over into his marriage proposal, telling his 14-stone girlfriend that he was prepared to marry only 10 stones of her. Rolf Schmidt told Isabel Witte that he would only marry her if she could fit into her old size 32 jeans, and she was apparently so desperate to marry this tolerant man that she even agreed to undergo cosmetic surgery to squeeze into those slimline jeans and get her man.

A Saudi man, aged 64, clocked up his 58th marriage last year, and said that he wasn't planning on stopping there, adding that he intended to take two more wives to 'round off his married life'. Saleh al-Saiari, a businessman, took a 13-year-old girl as his 58th wife, taking his harem up to the limit of four wives at a time, imposed by Islamic law. So to marry twice more, he will have to drop a couple of established wives from the squad. Saiari married for the first time at the age of 14, and his 58 marriages have so far produced 36 children.

DATING AND BEYOND

'Think of the positive side,' said Susan Schmidt at her office in Berlin. 'They are good-looking, guaranteed not to argue with you, promise to be there all the time, and don't leave dirty dishes, pick their noses, or argue over the TV remote control.' The perfect boyfriend or girl-friend, perhaps, apart from the fact that they are a little less than three-dimensional. Schmidt and her co-designer Andrea Baum created Singles wallpaper after reading about CDs that play everyday household sounds like toilets flushing and vacuum cleaners being used, so that people can pretend they are not alone in the house. Each fake friend on the Singles wallpaper acts out four different scenes – in the kitchen, living room, bathroom, and bedroom – so if you get the complete wallpaper set, you can have them in every room in your sad little flat.

A 71-year-old man met a 68-year-old woman through an online dating service in Guangzhou, in China. Nothing odd about that, really, except that in their online interactions he had been claiming to be 56

how not to get a date

Guys, read this and learn – you almost certainly won't get a hot date by whipping your willy out in public. You already knew that? Well, Joshua Baldwin, of Michigan, USA, tried this tactic around 16 times in a shopping centre before he was arrested and given 180 days in jail. He told police that he was only trying to meet women. 'I was only hoping to get lucky, but I went about it the wrong way,' Baldwin said, adding that he never thought it would bother anyone, and that he just assumed that women would enjoy the sight. He never got a date, though.

and the woman had been claiming to be 48. They chatted online for three months before agreeing to meet, but when the time came they were both so embarrassed at having lied about their ages that the man sent his son and the woman sent her daughter. The two children were forced to come clean, and the couple then met and decided to get married. We just hope they can trust each other.

NOOKIE

A homeless couple made an eye-catching protest against a lack of housing in Stockholm by getting into a bed in the middle of a city square, complete with a sign saying 'Even homeless people want to have sex.' And then they did just that, with an enthusiastic little crowd watching, for well over an hour until police arrived to break it up, so to speak.

Showing reckless abandon, little respect for convention and remarkable stamina, two men climbed high into a tree in New York's Central Park, stripped off and spent four hours sexing each other up in a variety of ways, screaming abuse at police and firefighters during their breaks from action. Eventually officers talked the couple, described as a transsexual with female breasts, wearing a purple thong, and a young man in white boxer shorts, out of the tree.

marital rights

A 43-year-old unemployed man had part of his benefits stopped when his wife, a native of Thailand, went back home for a while. He persisted with his benefit claim, on the grounds that since she could not afford to return to Germany, the government should pay for the travel; and since it refused to do that, it should pay him for at least four visits a month to a prostitute, plus an allowance to buy condoms, pornography and an appliance to aid masturbation. His claim was, astonishingly, rejected.

A female student auctioned her virginity on the Internet in order to avoid leaving university heavily in debt, and eventually found a buyer for £8,400. Rosie Reid – who is a lesbian – started the auction on eBay, but moved the sale to her own site, and faced a police investigation before she was able to go ahead with the sale. She met the five top bidders, assessed them over a ten-day period, then finally chose a 44-year-old man to pop her cherry.

An Australian man was fined A$100 after he was caught driving without a licence, but the reason he gave to police and at his appearance before a magistrate was priceless. Lee Collinson, of Northern Territory, was on a mercy mission to supply condoms to his cousin who was with a girl and ready to get jiggy with her. Magistrate David Loadman said: 'Carrying condoms to a mate who is in desperate need must be something much better than the good Samaritan ever did.'

OLD FOLKS

Old folks stubborn? You bet – try this for proof: an 86-year-old man from Bern in Switzerland headed off down the A6 motorway. The trouble was he set off down the wrong carriageway, against the flow of traffic. Did he realise he was going the wrong way? No, he was convinced *everyone else* was driving down the wrong carriageway, and he flashed his headlights continually at all those idiot drivers coming towards him. There were so many of these lunatics on the road, driving in the wrong direction, that when he spotted some police officers, he stopped to complain. The policemen swiftly confiscated the pensioner's car keys and drove him home.

You're never too old to defend your honour. An 85-year-old Chinese woman sued a neighbour who alleged that she wasn't a virgin – and won. The woman had been slandered, as she felt, in 1994, by a neighbour who said she had had secret affairs and since she was fiercely proud of reputation as an unsullied woman, she took the case to court, producing a doctor's certificate to prove her virginal status. After a protracted case the Huizhou Intermediate People's Court eventually awarded her damages of £150. And the neighbour was told to apologise.

A 66-year-old Dutchman was banned from using his local swimming pool because his overpowering body odour was too much for other customers to bear. The whiffy old geezer, who never wore anything other than the same unwashed shirt and trousers, was a regular three-times-a-week swimmer at the pool in the town of Rozenburg, and the management had been asking him to do something about his pong for over a year before the ban was eventually enforced, lasting for at least one year.

Blood was spilled in a Florida retirement home as three pensioners got stuck into each other in a fight over correct lettuce-serving technique. The ruck broke out at the Spring Haven Retirement Community, when a 62-year-old man took another man to task for using his hands, not the salad tongs, to serve himself lettuce at a mealtime, and continued with his harangue by punching him in the mouth. Another community resident piled in and at the end of it one of the men needed stitches in his head, one of them cut his arm and the third was bitten (good quality false teeth are quite sharp). Incredibly, the 62-year-old's mother was one of those trying to break the fight up.

At the grand old age of 84, Kenyan Kimani Murage, who has 30 grandchildren, enrolled at primary school. After the government made primary education free, Murage turned up at his local school and asked if

Eighty-four-year-old Romanian Auriel Blidaru was on his way to collect his pension in the town of Timisoara when he had a little accident. Auriel is registered as deaf and blind, so maybe he shouldn't have been driving, because he ran into a policeman, leaving him lying in the road with a broken leg. When patrol cars caught up with Mr Blidaru, he emerged from his car in dark glasses and carrying his white stick. He said he'd thought he'd sensed some kind of noise, but thought it was coming from the engine. Mr Blidaru added that he had been driving since 1950 without any problems, and since he knew the route and could see a tiny bit out of one eye, didn't think there was any harm in driving to collect his money. He added that he was planning to ask for his licence back and was prepared to resit his driving test if necessary.

ECCENTRIC

he could join, later arriving for his first class complete with school uniform. Murage hopes to become a vet, but his first goal was simply to learn to read.

DEATH – BREAKING UP IS HARD TO DO

Sometimes love doesn't die, even though the object of it does.

It was discovered this year that a man in northern China had been sleeping with his dead wife's corpse for the past eight years. Xie Yuchen's wife died of a cerebral haemorrhage in 1995 but he told neighbours that she was convalescing at home. The

A Venezuelan man didn't know what to do after his 103-year-old grandmother died. The 65-year-old from Caracas couldn't afford to pay for a funeral, so he tried to embalm her body himself. That didn't work, so he just put her in the fridge. But his attempt to keep the corpse fresh also failed, and eventually the smell of decomposing granny got to the neighbours, who called the police.

neighbours eventually suspected that all was not right, and called the police, who entered the house to find the mummified corpse in the marital bed. Her death had never been reported.

A Japanese couple ran away together against their parents' wishes, after they met on the Internet. While on the run, moving from hotel to hotel, they not only got married, but also conceived a child, which was stillborn. Fearing that reporting this to the authorities would lead to their parents finding them, Hitoshi Yoshikata, 37, and Minako Ito, 34, carried the dead baby in their luggage for five months. They were found out when they were arrested for failing to pay a hotel bill, and the dead baby's body was discovered wrapped in a towel inside a bag.

In rural western Ireland, a woman shared a room in her bungalow with her sister's corpse for possibly a year. 'Possibly' because Mary Ellen Lyons could not remember just when her sister Agnes died, and their brother, Michael, never entered his sisters' room. Agnes's body was discovered when Mary Ellen became ill and had to be taken to hospital, and it became clear that she had been sharing her bed with her dead sister, while Michael, who would not watch TV if there were women on it, such was the depth of his religious convictions, was never any the wiser.

Completely unable to accept the death of her husband, a Czech woman slept beside his corpse every night for almost two years. While spending each night alongside his dead body, the 67-year-old woman explained to neighbours that he was bedridden and unable to come downstairs during the day. Her explanations must have been convincing, because it was 18 months before the neighbours grew suspicious and tipped off the police.

After living with the corpse of his brother in another part of the mobile home they shared, 72-year-old Herbert Silver finally realised what had happened, and called the police. Although he announced his brother George's death as 'sudden' it was obviously not, and Herbert did admit that he had looked in on his brother in his bedroom from time to time, but to begin with saw nothing wrong. It was only when George appeared 'skeletal' that the penny dropped.

In this story, the mother of a 27-year-old woman sought outside help to deal with her daughter's death – but not any normal sort of assistance. The woman, from Kazakhstan, kept her daughter's mummified corpse in their apartment in the town of Pavlodar for three years, hoping that she would be brought back to life by aliens.

Here's a slight spin on the theme: a dog was shut up inside a cabin in Norway when his owner died. The man, who had no family, lay dead in the cabin for over a month before a neighbour investigated, to find that the dog had been surviving by eating the corpse of his beloved owner.

And another variant on the theme of staying with your dead loved one: a woman from the US state of Oklahoma was arrested by police in Florida after driving around with her mother's dead and decomposing body in the passenger seat. Police were called after shoppers at a 24-hour Wal-Mart complained about the stench emanating from a car in the car park, and when police located the woman inside the store, where she had been wandering around for some time, it emerged that she and her mother had driven together over the course of several weeks on a 1,300-mile road trip, during the course of which the mother had died of natural causes five days earlier, and the daughter just kept on moving on.

WEIRD DEATHS

Being too attached to material possessions can be a bad thing. Kevin McKeon, 25, of Taunton in Somerset, dropped his mobile phone down a drain as he walked home from a night at the pub. Assuming the distance below the drain cover to his lovely shiny mobile was about two feet, he prised up the cover and, on his hands and knees, tried to reach down inside. But it wasn't two feet down, it was six feet, and the drain was half full of water, so when McKeon overbalanced and fell forwards, he got stuck and drowned. He was discovered by a passer-by with his lifeless legs sticking up out of the drain. His mother was quoted as saying that as a child he had been taught to beware of drains.

Elaine Silcocks went to bed complaining of a pain in her left elbow, saying also that she just couldn't get warm. During the night she was sick several times. In the morning, her left elbow had swollen up – and her husband noticed two tiny puncture marks, only about a centimetre apart, on her right thigh. She said that they were old marks, but that she had no idea what they were. Jokingly, her husband suggested she had been bitten by a vampire; the doctor thought maybe it was an insect bite, but there was nothing further to indicate this. Whatever the tiny puncture wounds were – and Silcocks herself had no idea – they caused her to go into septic shock and she died eight days later.

When police broke into the house shared by a mother and son in Brighton, after being alerted by neighbours that something may have been wrong, they found that both Charlotte Major, 82, and her son, Clifford

Parsons, 45, were sitting slumped in armchairs, dead. Tests showed that the two died of natural causes within minutes of each other, Charlotte of a heart attack, and Clifford, a heavy drinker, of alcohol poisoning.

In a village near Shanghai, in China, an elderly woman was attacked by mice as she lay ill in bed. Her daughter came in from work to find her unconscious and covered with bite marks from mice, with her hands in particular very badly mauled. She later died from the injuries.

Now the city of Detroit has a bit of a reputation. The murder rate there runs at an average of one a day, so being killed by a flying bullet is not totally unexpected. But for Kimberley Mason, the passenger in a car driving down one of the city's streets at 2 a.m. one night, the bullet came from out of left-field, so to speak. Somewhere else in Detroit, someone shot into the air; the bullet went up and up, then down and down, piercing the car's roof and hitting her in the head, killing her.

During a car journey through their native Bangkok, a Thai father and son stopped to answer the call of nature. A few pertinent and weird details: it was pouring with rain; the son had a false leg, and he chose to

A Thai man was asleep one night, his wife beside him in bed, when he began to laugh. The 52-year-old man's wife awoke and then tried to wake him, but whatever was making him laugh in his sleep was just too funny, and she was unable to rouse him. After about two minutes of mirth, Damnoen Saen-um stopped breathing and died, apparently succumbing to heart failure. What a way to go.

horrible holiday homecoming

A couple living in New Mexico came home from a holiday to find their home was colder than it ought to have been. They went to the bathroom to see if the heating had been turned off, and saw a pair of legs protruding from the air conditioner duct. Further inspection revealed that the owner of the legs was the ex-husband of the woman and that he was dead. It looked as though he had been trying to break into the house from the roof and had got stuck in the duct.

urinate next to a power pole. Sadly for him his false leg on the wet ground acted as a conductor, his urine completed the circuit, and he was electrocuted.

DEATH AS ART

After long-term reconstruction work finally finished at the University of Arts in the Hungarian capital of Budapest, a garden building full of sculptures was seen to have a rather unusual piece of art added to it: a hanged man. For a whole day, people passing assumed this was a work of art until eventually the penny dropped: this was the real thing. After police

death as business

A Japanese undertaker took a golf club and beat his aunt to death with it because he needed the business. Not only was 42-year-old Nobuhiko Takahashi arrested for murder, but the funeral business went to a rival firm.

removed the hanging corpse it was estimated that it had been there about a year.

DESKBOUND DEATH

Now we have had to be careful checking this story, since there is an uncannily similar one in the 'Not true' section at the end of this book. We can never be 100 per cent sure but we think this really happened. A tax official in Helsinki died at his desk while checking tax returns (bored to death, we presume) and remained at his desk, unnoticed by colleagues, for two whole days. He died on a Tuesday, but no one realised that they were sharing their office with a corpse until the Thursday, despite the fact there were about 100 staff in his department.

JUST DESSERTS

Linda Maguire called the police during a domestic disturbance at their home in the US state of New Hampshire – she was being attacked by her husband, Bruce. When the police arrived, she had been stabbed several times by him, and he had then immediately suffered a fatal heart attack. She spent a night in the hospital. He spent the night in a morgue.

An 18-year-old man in the US state of Arkansas tried to drown his pet pit bull terrier. He wanted to kill it because it wasn't aggressive enough, and he tried to drown it, appropriately for a pit bull, in a pit of water. However, he fell in the pit and drowned, as did his father when he jumped in to save him. The dog escaped alive.

SUICIDE STORIES

This is one of the most pathetic stories we've heard for some time: a 23-year-old man in the US state of Maine tried to commit suicide by the highly dramatic method of self-crucifixion. He built a wooden cross especially for the purpose, then set to work. He first nailed one hand to the cross ... then realised that with one hand out of action he was unable to continue. He called the emergency services, although, as one of his rescuers said afterwards, whether it was for medical help or help in nailing the other hand onto the cross they weren't sure.

A tragic irony is at the root of this story from Tanzania. Samuel Boniface, 20, was looking after his boss's bicycle for him. While the bike was being looked after by Boniface, it was removed – stolen, he assumed. So he went to his employer to confess the bike had been stolen, then went to a cesspit and committed suicide by diving in and drowning himself in the effluent. A short time after his body was found floating in the cesspit, the bike was returned by a friend who had borrowed it for a little while.

It's a dangerous game to play ... A young Taiwanese man, Huang Tzu-Heng, decided to test the strength of his girlfriend's love for him. He emailed her, posing as 'Mr J.', and began an online relationship with her, while the couple continued to go out with each other. Soon, she told him that she wanted to split up with him because she had fallen in love with Mr J. Tzu-Heng went home and killed himself; his suicide note explained that he and Mr J. were one and the same.

A 32-year-old Tanzanian man took the ultimate escape route after the constant nagging of his wife became too much for him to bear. Apparently unwilling

The Minister for Works and Transport in Botswana came out with a piece of advice for prospective Botswanan suicides: don't jump in front of a train – jump from a tree instead. 'If people want to commit suicide they should use trees not our trains,' said Ms Tebelelo Seretse, pointing out that train drivers found it rather traumatic. She has offered counselling to drivers who have dealt with suicides.

ODD

to consider leaving her or throwing her out, he drank a chemical used in cattle dips and left a suicide note explaining that his wife's tongue had driven him to this.

 A Frenchman took out the entire contents of his bank account in cash, dumped the banknotes, with a value of about £170,000, into the bath and set them alight. He then swallowed two bottles of pills; the idea was to kill himself and leave nothing behind. His plan was foiled by neighbours, who saw smoke coming from his house and alerted the emergency services. Saved from death, he faced life with no funds whatsoever – but was reported to be looking forward to starting a new life.

In Dar-es-Salaam, capital of Tanzania, a woman saved her husband from death after she had

Aren't lawyers supposed to be clever? New York lawyer Larry Feingold, 53, came to trial last year after trying to commit suicide in his apartment by turning on the gas. The explosion that happened when it ignited took out three whole floors of the building. Feingold said he didn't know gas could explode. Gasoline, yes, he knew that one, he said, but gas, no.

caught him in bed with another woman. The 35-year-old man decided to hang himself after being found out, rather than have it known he was an adulterer, but his wife cut him down. While recovering in hospital he was waiting to be charged with attempted suicide, which is a crime in Tanzania.

TALES FROM THE CRYPT

The family of Belgian Marc Marchal got a shock as they were gathered round his coffin, saying their last farewell to the 32-year-old, killed in a motorcycle crash. The undertakers had decided to put his body straight into his coffin, since it was badly damaged from the crash, rather than lay it out for the farewell. As the mourners stood around his coffin, a mobile phone started ringing. It became quickly apparent that the offending phone was inside the coffin – in Marc's jacket. Disgusted mourners left the chapel of rest while the undertakers had to open the coffin and remove the phone from the dead man's pocket.

Passers-by in a Chinese cemetery were astonished to hear music drifting up from the ground. Investigations revealed that the relatives of a man who loved his music had buried him with his radio, switched on and tuned to his favourite music station.

Planning – or plotting – ahead ... A pub owner in Saddleworth, Greater Manchester, bought some land near his hostelry and got planning permission to turn it into a cemetery with space for 8,000 people. And it wasn't long before regulars at the Church Inn were buying plots of land along with their pints and pies, and the landlord's Auntie Evelyn is already buried there. One regular who bought a plot has asked his friends from the pub to pop into the cemetery with their pints on Friday nights after he dies, so that he can still have a drink with his pals.

The tradition in Brazil at a funeral is that just before the coffin goes into the earth, it is opened to give the grieving relatives one last chance to see their beloved. So when the coffin of a woman, Reinivalda Sacramento, was opened to show her relatives the body, and there was the corpse of a man there, there was a bit of a to-do, with some relatives fainting at the sight. It turned out that the man had died on the same day at the same hospital and had got put in the coffin, while Sacramento's body had been left at the hospital (and would have ended up in the dead man's coffin at his funeral).

Thanks to his caring daughter, who managed to track down the perfect vehicle, 68-year-old Dennis Lloyd of West Yorkshire, who was a mad keen motorcycle fanatic, was transported to his funeral in a hearse that was actually the sidecar of a specially adapted Triumph motorbike.

In a pagoda in northern Vietnam, a monk was found sitting in the lotus position, as all good Buddhist monks should. The weird difference was that this particular monk had been sitting there for 280 years. The corpse of the monk, Nhu Tri, who died in 1723 in a tower at the Tieu Pagoda in Bac Ninh province, was covered in a layer of special preservative paint. His internal organs remained intact but one eye socket was damaged and his arms were broken off at the elbow.

A champion Irish clay pigeon shooter had his dying wish granted – to go out with a bang. Tony Mullan, who died aged 63 after a long illness, asked his friends to pack his ashes into cartridges and shoot them over firing ranges around the world. Mullan's oldest friend and shooting colleague, Willie Hughes, emptied 50 cartridges of lead, replaced them with tightly packed ashes, and fires one off at every firing range he goes to.

BIZARRE

It's almost as though they'd been following *Another Weird Year*, and noting the incidences of corpses turning out to be still alive ... A cemetery in Santiago, Chile, started offering 'smart' coffins that can spot signs of life to avoid the unpleasantness of burying a living but helpless person. The sensor detects movement inside the coffin, so that in the case of catalepsy, for example, in which total paralysis can be mistaken for death, the individual can be saved from real death. Surely better to get a second medical opinion, though, than bury someone in a sensor-rigged coffin? But as the cemetery spokesperson said, presumably hoping to sell lots of very expensive coffins, 'We want families to rest assured that if a case like this ever happens their loved ones will be immediately rescued.'

When my cat died last year (sniff, sniff) the vet kindly arranged for his body to be taken away from the surgery and disposed of, which took place in another town. Fine for cats, but would this be acceptable for humans? Well, the phenomenon of 'corpse tourism' emerged last year in Germany, thanks to rapidly rising funeral costs. The bodies of deceased loved ones are sent to Poland or the Czech Republic to be cremated, and it's cheaper than having it done at home.

You can choose your friends, but you can't choose your family. And you wouldn't choose families like these ...

In the last edition of *Another Weird Year* you read about Alison Greenhowe in Scotland, then 19, and her brand-new husband George, 20, moving in with Alison's mother Pat, and Alison finding her husband George in bed with her mother Pat, and Pat and George getting married, so that Alison's ex-husband became her stepfather. Well, the following year, things carried on being interestingly weird in Alison's life. She started courting again, but four days before her wedding to Peter Knight, 28, he told his bride-to-be – eight months pregnant, by the way – that he wasn't going to marry her. Nice. And he gallantly told her by text message. Classy, very classy. But wait. In those four days that lay between being dumped and her wedding day, Alison got back with another ex, Daniel Innes, 18, and after changing the names on the wedding invitations and ordering a different-sized kilt for the groom, the wedding went ahead, just with a different bloke. Daniel was OK about not definitely being the father, although apparently he was one of three possible candidates Alison slept with around the same time – first fiancé Peter Knight, or Daniel Innes, or Daniel's brother.

Here's a tale of reunion and dishonesty that would grace a Greek tragedy. George Potter's dad left his mum when he was a baby, but 20 years later George made the effort to trace his father, also called George, and found him. The two got on well, and quickly became firm friends. George Jnr introduced his dad to the people close to him, including his fiancée Mary-Anne, while George Snr introduced his son to his new wife Sandra. Then this cosy little family scene was ripped to shreds when George Jnr received a phone call from a neighbour telling him to go home immediately. He burst into his house to find his long-lost dad in bed with his fiancée. George Snr's wife, Sandra, filed for divorce after being cheated on by her prospective daughter-in-law, and George Jnr and Mary-Anne are no longer engaged to be married.

In the Canadian city of Winnipeg, a 40-year-old man and his 16-year-old son, who just happened to be carrying a loaded shotgun, were walking home. On a whim, apparently, they decided to rob some passing pedestrians of the beer they were carrying. There was a fight, the beer was not handed over to the wantonly violent family, and the son accidentally shot the father.

THE CONTRARIEST VOW OF SILENCE

Angered by his father's opposition to his becoming an artist, Rainer Herpel of Bad Ems in Germany vowed never to speak until his father was no more. He refused to work in his father's shoe shop and concentrated on his paintings. He lived with his mother, and always ate alone – subsisting on hamburgers – and whenever he was out he wore covers over his ears so that he would not be spoken to. Last year, Rainer's father died, and after 29 years of silence, he finally spoke. Sadly, we don't know what his first words were.

Jeremy Kingston, a resident of Salt Lake City, lives in a community where family life can get kinda complicated. He was jailed for marrying 15-year-old Lu-Ann Kingston, who was not only his (under-age) wife, but also his cousin. And his aunt too. Like I said, it's a complicated family.

More complex family ties: a British woman gave birth to her own stepbrother. Carole Moore, 29, acted as a surrogate mother for Maureen Knight, 52, married to Ms Moore's stepfather, Harry Knight, who donated the sperm.

FAMILIES REUNITED

When 48-year-old Bob Kunath of Orlando, Florida, saw an old cookie jar at a flea market, he liked it but thought the price was too steep; so he went home and found a similar one on the eBay website for much less money. When he took delivery of the jar, he spotted the seller's name – Saylor. Bob Kunath, who was an adopted child, knew his biological father's name was Harry Saylor, and he lived in New Jersey – where the seller also lived. So Bob called up the seller, who turned out to be his very own brother – who happens to deal in the same retro-style cookie-jar artists that Bob so loves.

In 1997, in Philadelphia, Luz Cuevas lost her ten-day-old baby daughter in a house fire. In January 2004, she was at a children's birthday party and she saw a little girl who looked exactly as though she could be her own daughter. Ms Cuevas was so convinced that she was looking at her daughter that she took some hair from the little girl's head, on the pretence that there was some chewing gum in it, and had it tested for DNA. The result? Ms Cuevas's maternal instinct was correct – it was indeed her daughter. The authorities believe that a family acquaintance snatched the baby one night and created a fire to make it look as though the baby was dead. At the time of the fire, it was believed that the baby's body had been totally destroyed by the intense heat and flames. Ms Cuevas had her suspicions even then, since the bedroom window, normally shut as it was winter, was wide open, and especially since the acquaintance, Carolyn Correa, announced she was pregnant, and also ceased all contact with Cuevas after the fire, but her fears were put down to post-traumatic stress. After the DNA test, Correa was wanted on charges of arson and kidnapping.

Eleven years ago, in West Bengal, a little boy was bitten by a poisonous snake. The family of eight-year-old Subash Bag believed that the bite had killed him, and in keeping with ancient tradition, placed his body on a raft and launched it down the Damodar River. When the raft eventually ran aground, an old man rescued the boy, and after many days of treatment the little boy was well again, although without any memory of where he had come from. Subash Bag grew up, married and had a daughter, and eleven years later was in the market of his home town when he was recognised by a relative, who told Bag's father. The father travelled to see his son, and was reunited with the boy who came back from the dead.

A 60-year-old man from Barnsley, in South Yorkshire, found out his family set-up was not what he thought. In fact, Mick Henry discovered that he was the chief of a Canadian native Indian tribe. One day he received an email – completely out of the blue – telling him he had a brother called Sitting Eagle and a sister called Thunder Woman living on a reservation near Winnipeg. Mr Henry's father, who had been chief of the Ojibway people, had married an Englishwoman while serving in Britain during the Second World War. The marriage didn't last, Mr Henry's father went back to Canada, and his mother never told him that his father was a native Canadian Indian. After the death of his father, Mr Henry inherited the title of chief; he went to see his people, danced round a fire, did a bit of chanting, and returned to South Yorkshire with a new outlook on life.

PARENTING

It's nice to take an active interest in your children's hobbies, maybe help them to get better at them, that sort of thing. But there are limits. Florida police were forced to haul in April Marie Brown after she was caught driving her twelve-year-old son and one of his cute little pals around town one Saturday night so that they could vandalise street signs.

I remember being a sulky, disobedient teenager and I'm sure my mum despaired of me. But even in her dreams (I hope!) she never contemplated going to the lengths that Olga Iliokina went to when her disobedient son was hard to deal with. Iliokina hired one of her twelve-year-old son's schoolmates to kill him, offering him the princely sum of £20 for the hit. Iliokina, 32, told the court in Orenburg that she was sick of her son's refusal to do as he was told and decided to have him killed. The 14-year-old hitman suffocated the boy, and was arrested after the body was discovered. He received a nine-year prison sentence, while the mother got 20 years.

Melissa Wright, 27, of Alabama, received a 25-year jail sentence for putting her 18-month-old daughter into a hot oven. She told authorities that she was holding the baby in her arms when she opened the oven to check on some liver she was cooking, and the child slipped from her arms, fell on the door, rolled into the oven and the door closed.

Giving birth six times is not unusual. But when each pregnancy produces triplets, then that is a bit weird. Fatma Saygi, 28, from the Turkish province of Adiyaman, gave birth to her sixth set of triplets last year. Her husband Mehmet, a wedding singer who earns about £12 a week, was said to be 'happy' at the birth of kids numbers 16, 17 and 18.

What are the chances of this happening? The odds on any four women in one area having children on the same date would be fairly long, but if those four women were sisters? Any bookmaker would be happy to give you very generous odds on that, but New Zealander Pauline Te Wiki and her three sisters proved that it is possible. Ms Te Wiki gave birth to her son Ngawhai Te Wiki in a New Zealand hospital on 11 March, the same date three of her sisters have had babies in previous years. Little Ngawhai shares his birth date with cousins Jahreece, three, Waimarie, 13, and Stacy, 14.

A 40-year-old woman in a remote, rural area of Mexico went into labour and then realised that she was in difficulties. Having lost a previous baby due to labour complications, she took the hard decision to give herself a Caesarean. The woman downed a couple of shots of strong alcohol, then sliced herself open with a kitchen knife, delivering a healthy baby boy. As she started to lapse into unconsciousness, she managed to instruct one of her children to call a local nurse for help, who stitched up the opening with a sewing needle and cotton, and her life was saved. This appears to be the first known case of a self-performed Caesarean in which both the mother and baby survived.

Terry Lee Crouch, of Florida, and his six-year-old son had a great game they used to play. They would drive out to a dirt road, and Crouch's son would hang on to the rear bumper of their car while Crouch drove the car backwards and forwards, trying to shake

A Brazilian ex-couple got one hell of a shock when they took DNA tests. Tereza Menas and her former boyfriend were tested when their nine-year-old daughter wanted her father's name to be put on her birth certificate. Although the man had indeed fathered a baby with Tereza, the tests showed that neither one of them was the biological parent of the girl: it was believed that hospital staff had swapped Tereza's baby with another one born the same day.

ODD

him off. Great game, until Crouch ran over his son, causing him severe facial injuries.

A Chinese couple brought up their only child for 13 years as a girl, simply because they thought she was one. The child had had underdeveloped sex organs at birth, which led them to assume the baby was female, but strange reactions down there at the sight of pretty women on TV caused them to take their daughter to hospital where the truth – and, after a simple and successful operation, the male genitals – emerged.

KIDS

The US state of Montana is one of the last outposts of the Wild West. And in the small community of Forsyth, two eight-year-old boys proved it by bringing a loaded handgun and a knife to school, burying them in the playground sandpit and planning to stab and shoot a classmate during playtime. Their intended victim was a girl who had teased them. Fortunately for everyone another eight-year-old alerted teachers (or 'told tales' if you prefer) and the kids were arrested.

'Show and tell' day is always a fun part of primary schooling. But in a primary school in Darwin, Australia, there was a shock in store for teachers when

A child prodigy was noticed in the US state of Louisiana, where the Formosa Gardens restaurant had a two-year-old boy working on the cash register. Little Gordon Tan can also work the credit card machine. Gordon climbs up on a chair, takes the cash from the diners, rings up the totals on the machine and gives them the correct change. Despite being only a couple of months past his second birthday he was able to tell credit and debit cards apart. One family dines regularly at the restaurant, apparently, just to watch him in action.

Was this a case of mistaken identity or a kid copying his parents' habit of combining mealtimes with a cannabis buzz? A five-year-old boy in Florida was caught sprinkling marijuana over a classmate's lasagne at school lunch, just before the classmate started eating it. The boy apparently said it was oregano, but the fact that he tried to hide the bag of dope with his feet suggested that he knew what it was.

a five-year-old girl brought in a Coke bottle and showed her little classmates how to make it into a bong for smoking cannabis.

Meanwhile, in the US city of Indianapolis, a four-year-old boy brought crack cocaine worth around $10,000 to his preschool class. The boy took rocks of crack cocaine out of his backpack and showed them to other children in his Head Start class, saying the drugs were flour, but the teachers realised it was cocaine and called the police.

TEENS

Give 'em an inch and they'll take your house. A 16-year-old boy in the American city of Cincinnati held a week-long series of parties while his father and stepmother were away. At the end of the week the damage to the $380,000 house was so great that he felt that the only way to conceal the carnage was to burn the house down.

A Spanish schoolteacher gave his whole administration and finance class at Parque Aluche college top marks after they formed a political party to explore how democracy works, and ended up winning nearly 70,000 votes in the Spanish general election. The students' Accion Yuntar Party was the fifth most popular in the race for Madrid's four Senate seats, despite it having only 19 members, almost no campaign funds and a classroom as its headquarters.

Three Czech schoolboys used their horticulture classes to grow marijuana, brazenly and right under the noses of their teachers. The teachers at the school in Rymarov, in the north-east Czech Republic, thought the boys had been growing tomato plants, and encouraged them in their new-found enthusiasm for horticulture lessons. That lasted until they were caught smoking the 'tomato' leaves, and the police were called in. The boys should get full marks for originality in school horticulture.

Seventeen-year-old Carlos Chereza was charged in Florida with taking out a contract on his own mother. Unfortunately for him, the hitman he hired, with an offer of $2,000, and to whom he gave a plan of his apartment, the keys to it and a picture of his mother, was an undercover policeman. Chereza, who thought he would inherit his mother's money, showed just what his priorities were when he asked the hitman to make sure the TV didn't get damaged by bullets.

not kids

In Galena, Illinois, authorities were called in to investigate a very strange case indeed. A 13-year-old boy, Chris Gomez, tried to enrol in a middle school by asking a pastor at a Galena church for help. The boy said he'd been the victim of child abuse. After noticing a few inconsistencies in the boy's story the pastor confronted him, and the 'boy' admitted to being a 33-year-old woman with three children.

FISHFINGER ON THE TRIGGER

Deep in the heart of gun country, a Texas woman put on her oven to heat up some fishfingers, little knowing that a friend of hers had stashed a gun there for safe-keeping. It wasn't long before the oven got hot enough to explode the bullets, and several rounds of fire shot out of the oven, catching Roxanne Perez in the leg.

DIVINE RETRIBUTION

Now I hope there aren't KKK members reading this who know where to find me, but here's a case of them getting what they deserve. At a Ku Klux Klan initiation ceremony in the US state of Tennessee, Jeffrey Murr was being inducted into this revolting organisation. Tied to a tree, he was shot with paintball guns, while a KKK member fired a pistol into the air to make the shooting sound realistic. The pistol bullet went up, up, up, and came down with unerring precision onto the head of Murr, passing through his skull and seriously injuring him. Gregory Freeman, 45, who fired the bullet, fled the ceremony but was soon caught by the police near his home.

AUTO-AMPUTATIONS

A farmer in the Canadian province of Saskatchewan got his thumb and little finger caught in a stone-picking machine. Out there in the fields, with no one to hear him scream, Bruce Osiowy remained for 66 hours, at which point he decided that he had better take things into his own hands. Or hand. He used his Swiss Army knife to cut off the thumb and finger, and then was able to drive his tractor back to his farmhouse to call for medical help.

Deep underground in an Australian coal mine, 43-year-old Colin Jones rolled his tractor on a sharp bend, trapping his right arm against the wall of a tunnel. Worried that leaking fuel from his vehicle would cause an explosion, he begged his workmate to cut his arm off so that they could quickly move on. His workmate wasn't too keen, so Jones got on with it himself, even though the emergency rescuers had been alerted. Jones set about his arm with his Stanley knife and cut off the crushed part of the limb below the elbow. His workmate packed it in a plastic bag and helped Jones back up to the surface, where he was rushed to hospital. Surgeons were unable to reattach the limb, so

Jones was faced with the terrible misfortune of having to give up playing the banjo.

Every year it seems someone gets their head cut off. Last year it was an Indian man in the state of Uttar Pradesh, a 28-year-old who crashed into a truck and was almost entirely decapitated by a metal rod. The man tied his head back on with a piece of cloth, and with his eyes popping out of his head and blood everywhere, drove 18 miles to a hospital in Agra, where he lost consciousness. His direct action saved his life, and two weeks later he was on the road to recovery.

Somanath Bahinipati, of Orissa, in India, was using a scythe to trim plants in his garden when he hit a cobra. The poisonous snake immediately coiled itself around his left hand, and Bahinipati was unable to shake it off. He realised he had a very sharp and dangerous tool in his right hand – but instead of using the scythe on the snake, he decided that the best course of action was to hack off his left hand. Bahiniapati was not bitten by the snake, but lost copious amounts of blood, as well as most of his hand.

STUCK!

'Oh dear, what can the matter be ...?' A Canadian woman spent two days wedged behind her toilet at her home in Winnipeg. The elderly woman told paramedics that she couldn't remember how she had managed to get stuck there, but her whole body was completely jammed behind the toilet, to the extent that firemen were called in to smash the porcelain so that she could be removed.

A New York man was trapped in his apartment for two days beneath a pile of newspapers, magazines, catalogues and junk mail. Patrice Moore, 43, who sells books and magazines on the street, was discovered when his landlord came to the apartment and heard a weirdly muffled voice calling from inside. Moore's apartment was crammed with all manner of paper and reading matter, collected over a ten-year period and stacked up from floor to ceiling. One of the massive stacks collapsed on him, pinning him down completely. It took emergency services half an hour to free him, and 50 rubbish bags of papers were removed after his rescue. At least he had something to read while he was waiting.

DRUNKENNESS

People worry about legalising cannabis and other drugs, when one of the most lethal and behaviour-altering drugs is out there, guaranteed to produce weird results all over the world. Alcohol.

Two Bosnian brothers who said they were always able to knock back as much booze as they wanted and never get drunk, nor suffer hangovers, found out the reason why last year. Josip Galic, 69, had a car accident and while in hospital it was discovered that he had four kidneys instead of the regulation two. And his brother Ante visited the doctor to be told that he, too, had a massive kidney surplus. In both cases all the kidneys were fully functioning. **ODD**

Deep in the Australian state of Northern Territory, Gordon Lyons was driving with a friend from the town of Mandorah to the state capital, Darwin. He admitted to being very drunk – which was partly why, when he saw a king brown snake, one of Australia's deadliest, by the side of the road, he decided to pick it up as a souvenir for his local pub back in Mandorah. Unwilling to put down the can of beer in his right hand, Lyons made the mistake of grabbing the snake with his left. The snake easily wriggled loose and promptly bit him in his hand. Lyons grabbed it again, slung it in a plastic bag and dropped the bag into his car before his mate set off again for Darwin, this time heading for the hospital. So drunk was Lyons, though, that during the journey he put his hand back inside the bag, and was bitten another eight times. He became very seriously ill almost immediately, and lost consciousness just before he was taken to hospital. His mate tried to keep him awake during the journey by pouring beer on his head. Lyons had so much venom in his body that he spent seven weeks in a coma, and so much venom in his left arm that it had to be amputated. Now that IS a drinking session!

A man with nearly four times the permitted level of alcohol in his bloodstream, as tests later revealed, managed in the space of ten short yards and a few short seconds, to do £150,000 worth of damage with his car. Leslie Arliss of Bradford came home from the pub a little worse for wear and decided that he wanted his car parked a little closer to his house. He should have left well alone, because after lurching into his 4-litre Range Rover to move it ten yards closer to home, he hit a total of eleven cars, flipping one over onto its roof. That's more than one car damaged per yard driven. Arliss explained it all away by telling the police his foot had got trapped between the brake and accelerator pedals. More like his head got stuck in a beer barrel.

The winner of a drinking competition in Russia received his trophy in heaven, since the effect of downing several pints of vodka was death by alcohol poisoning. There were five other contestants, and they were all taken to hospital for emergency treatment for severe alcohol poisoning. The competition was held in a bar in the Volgodonsk region and the prize for the winner was ten bottles of vodka. During the event each man knocked back several pint glasses of vodka, which were topped up from buckets filled to the brim. They were allowed under the rules of the contest to eat black bread, sausage and mustard.

SELF-EATING

Yes, that's right, people eating bits of themselves. The posh word is autophagy, in case you didn't know.

Beset by a mad case of the munchies after sniffing butane gas, an Austrian man with nothing to eat in the house took a kitchen knife, sliced the toes off his left foot and chucked them in a frying pan. He was munching on a fried toe sandwich when his sister came into the kitchen and then called the police. The man generously offered the officers a bite of his sandwich as he was hauled away, and told the ambulance man that he had more toes than he needed anyway.

Same part of the body, different reason. A Romanian serving a prison sentence for car theft discovered that his girlfriend had got married to another man. So he sliced off both his little toes and ate them raw, then cut some of his thigh off, fried it and ate it. Neculai Berariu said he wanted to shock people, but that he'd never do it again.

THINGS INSIDE YOU THAT REALLY SHOULDN'T BE

A 42-year-old Chinese man was admitted to hospital in Luoding, having recently developed a mental disorder. When surgeons took a look at what was going on inside his brain, it was hardly surprising that he had gone a bit nuts. There was a 3.5-inch worm living there. Experts suggested that the man's habit of eating frogs and snakes may have introduced the worm into his system.

In West Bengal, an eleven-year-old boy told his uncle that he could see things coming out of the corner of his eye. Abu Bakkar's uncle was sceptical until he noticed a sore on the boy's eye, which he rubbed with some cotton wool, upon which a small procession of ant-like creatures emerged and crawled away.

Taking the agricultural life to its limits, a Romanian boy was discovered to have a plant growing in his nose. The four-year-old boy, from a mountain village in Vrancea county, had only been taken to see the doctor

A young girl from Costa Rica was taken to hospital complaining of tummy ache. Doctors decided to operate when they realised that there was something fairly large inside her. The cause of the stomach pains was a massive hairball, measuring 17 inches and weighing one and a half pounds. No one in her family knew that the girl was in the habit of eating her own hair.

for a routine check-up, but there in his nose was a bean that had germinated and sprouted leaves.

Two levels of 'things inside you' in this story: a 73-year-old Taiwanese woman had for 53 years suffered a lot of pain whenever she had sex. The woman had had a baby delivered by Caesarian section in 1949, and the midwife had left a needle inside her after sewing her up. Finally, after years of a poking pain, a CT scan revealed a rusty needle in her vagina.

A report in an Indian medical journal described the following case. A 27-year-old woman had a cough that simply would not stop, and was sent for an

An Israeli woman was cleaning her house when a cockroach jumped into her mouth and crawled down her throat. The 32-year-old woman immediately tried to hook the intruding beast out with a fork, but that got lodged in her throat too and she swallowed it. She was operated on in hospital to have the fork removed, which came out without any difficulty, but the cockroach had already been digested and had passed on to a better place.

X-ray. The X-ray revealed a condom lodged in the upper area of her lung. Confronted with the evidence, the woman admitted that she knew it was there and that she had accidentally swallowed it while carrying out fellatio.

MAKING A MESS OF YOUR GENITALS ...

For many people – and it seems to be men, frankly – genitals seem to be more trouble than they're worth. Read these stories, chaps, and shudder.

Now if ever there was a lesson to be learned about the perils of hallucinogenic drugs, this is it. A Malaysian man who had taken some pills before he went to sleep woke up hearing voices urging him to do things to his body, those things being to slice off his own penis, fry it and eat it. All of which he dutifully carried out. The 34-year-old realised what he had done when he beheld his blood-soaked crotch, and called for help.

An Australian man was apparently copying a stunt seen on a TV programme on practical jokes, by walking across a room with a lit firework between the cheeks of his buttocks. Unfortunately, the 26-year-old slipped backwards, falling onto his backside as the firecracker exploded. The result was a fractured pelvis, haemorrhaging from the buttocks, as well as severe genital burns and, worst of all, a ruptured urethra, leaving him incontinent and sexually dysfunctional.

A Cambodian man was visited in a dream, so he said, by four hungry spirits, and the problem was that he had no chicken or duck to offer them to appease their hunger. But he could offer them his penis, to which the spirits apparently agreed. Quite when the dream turned into reality, we cannot say, but he promptly whipped off his genitals with a butcher's knife. He was rushed to a hospital near the capital Phnom Penh, where his life was saved by medics.

Staying with the **UNUSUAL** fireworks-groin link, a man in Jacksonville, Florida, tried to throw a commercial firework from his car at his girlfriend after a row. Shannon Kramer badly misjudged the time it would take for the fuse to burn down, which was half a second rather than several seconds, and since he was holding the firework between his legs, it all went rather nastily wrong for him. Neighbours ran to the car and used a fire extinguisher to douse his flaming groin, but nor before he had suffered serious burns.

Back to the weird link between hallucinogens and making a sorry mess of your love gear. An 18-year-old German student was just being part of a craze that was sweeping Germany, of drinking a tea made with angels' trumpet plants, a known hallucinogen. According to his mother, the young man was behaving normally until he went out into the garden for a little while. He returned having cut off not only his penis, but his tongue too. When the emergency services arrived they saw that he had used garden shears to do the cutting, making such a good job of it that there was no chance of reattaching either organ.

Talk about attention-seeking behaviour. A Tanzanian man cut off his genitals in an attempt to soften the hearts of his creditors. The 24-year-old man had borrowed large sums of money to invest in a business venture, but had frittered it all away on prostitutes and booze. When he realised that he was unable to pay back the loans, he chopped off his genitals in a bid for sympathy. He was treated in hospital. At least he won't be spending any more money on prostitutes now.

Proof that you shouldn't try at home what you see in the movies. A 49-year-old Romanian man slid an industrial nut over his penis to try and maintain an erection, after watching an actor do so in a porn film. His penis began to swell and swell, until the nut (and his

Firemen in Moscow spent a whole hour freeing a Russian man's penis from a padlock, where he had put it for a bit of kinky fun. They succeeded in cutting the padlock off but doctors said that the man's penis would be bent over to one side for the rest of his life. Literally kinky.

nuts) was barely visible. The surgeon tasked with dealing with the problem was considering having to amputate, until he hit on the idea of making a few vertical slices in the organ to drain the blood off and shrink the man's penis.

... AND OF OTHER PEOPLE'S ...

A court case this year revealed a sad situation that had occurred a couple of years earlier in Texas. Hurshell Ralls, 67, went into hospital for bladder surgery and woke up after his operation to discover his penis was missing. Ralls had been down for surgery on his bladder because he had cancer, and during the operation the surgeons decided that the cancer had spread to his penis, and removed it. Ralls's lawyer contended that he had not given permission to have his penis amputated and had not been told that he would wake up without it.

A touching family moment here: a woman in Vietnam, when faced with an unfaithful husband, enlisted the help of their 17-year-old son to deal with the matter. He helped tie up his father, while she took to his naughty bits with a large knife, cutting off the offending organ. Neighbours took the man to hospital, but it was too late for his penis to be reattached.

... AND OF OTHER BODY PARTS

I'm assuming the two men involved here heard about the case, reported in an earlier edition of *Another Weird Year*, of an Italian bleeding to death after having his leg chainsawed off to claim insurance, or it may simply have been a good example of German efficiency and thoroughness. Two Germans were convicted of insurance fraud after it was discovered that they had staged a chainsaw accident, in which one of the men had his thumb and forefinger lopped off. He then threw away the fingers and claimed from two separate insurers, profiting to the tune of €40,000. It was carefully done, with one man holding onto a cutting board, while his accomplice started up the chainsaw and trimmed his finger complement down from ten to eight. After going through all that pain it seems understandable to want to boast about it, but it was this that led to their arrest.

It's no good meaning well if you get it wrong. Badly wrong, in the case of a school janitor in Portugal, trying to help a 14-year-old schoolboy after the boy had hurt himself in a fall. The janitor applied alcohol to the injured leg then set it alight. Antonio Pereira was treated for first- and second-degree burns after being told by the janitor that that was what they used to do in the war. 'I told him I wasn't in a war,' said the boy.

PROBLEMS WITH POINTY THINGS

When an argument between neighbours, in Thatcham, Berkshire, escalated into violence, Matthew Hawkins, 15, was shot in the face with a harpoon gun. The harpoon had three barbed points which pierced his eye socket, cheek and jaw. One point was just one milli-metre away from severing an artery and causing his death. Matthew had to wait for 14 hours – wide awake – while surgeons decided how best to remove the barbs from his skull without killing him. Then there was the operation itself, another seven hours, followed by a second operation to remove his damaged eye. From being one millimetre away from death to full recovery took less than three weeks.

Mary Hughes, 65, stumbled down the stairs of her home in Manchester and landed on the tip of a snooker cue left at the bottom of the stairs by her husband. The cue pierced the left side of her neck and emerged from her right cheek, just missing her windpipe and several fairly important arteries. She was fine once some friendly firemen cut the cue from her head.

Doctors in China successfully removed a trio of pointy things from a man's head. The man, named Guo, had three sewing needles embedded in his brain for 29 years, and his parent had not the slightest idea how they came to be there. The surgeons theorised that they must have been inserted there when he was a

Surgeons in the Malaysian city of Ipoh were treating a man for an eye infection, and were astounded to discover that there was part of a wooden chopstick embedded in his face. Not only that, but it had been there, along with a tiny portion of spare rib, for five whole years. The surgeons reported that the pointed end of the chopstick was just about in contact with his brain, and that he had been about half a centimetre from death. The man, a car park attendant, had been attacked and stabbed with the chopstick five years earlier, but it was only when an infection set in that he sought medical help, and discovered what the cause was.

QUIRKY

baby, when the skull was soft enough to allow needles to penetrate it. Guo found out he had three needles in there after an X-ray in 1994, but no doctor was prepared to attempt the dangerous operation of removing them until last year, when surgeons at the 999 Hospital in southern China used a new system involving a microscope and a magnet to fish the needles out of his brain, and Guo has been fine ever since.

MISTAKEN IDENTITY

Council employees in Schieder-Schwalenberg, Germany, were called out to fell an ash tree that grew in front of one of Germany's most famous and beloved trees, a 500-year-old oak, because the ash was making it difficult for art students to paint or photograph the magnificent oak. With typical efficiency a team of tree fellers was sent out, and they swiftly levelled the ash to the ground. The next day, due to a mix-up, another team was sent out to do the same job, and finding only one tree in the location, felled it and then rendered it into firewood-sized chunks. This, as you will have guessed, was the magnificent 500-year-old oak, the national treasure that art students painted and that made local residents glow with pride.

In the Scottish county of Fife, Marion Garry called a team of archaeologists to her house, when, after watching a TV programme about hidden archaeological wonders, she wondered if some slabs of stone in her back garden were of significance. Very much so, was the verdict of the team of archaeologists: this was clearly a ninth-century Viking village, possibly the earliest on mainland Scotland, and the slabs had obviously been hauled up from a beach nearby. The presence of a Second World War gas mask did not stop them from clearing the whole area, at which point it became evident that the gem of a Norse village was no more than a 1940s patio.

WHOOPS!

Silly mistakes can cost you dearly.

A Brazilian football referee, Carlos Jose Figueira Ferro, reached into his pocket for his red card during a match in the city of Anama, to send off footballer Paulo Coise. Into his pocket went his hand, and out of his pocket came a pair of red lacy knickers. His wife happened to be watching the match, and divorce proceedings followed soon afterwards.

Spare a thought for the colleague of a construction worker in New York City. The worker was buried up to his neck when a trench collapsed, just his head sticking up. The colleague decided, while waiting for emergency crews to arrive, to try and dig his mate out.

It's good to help the police, but important to get your facts right. A motorist phoned the police in Bavaria to say that he had just seen a man driving along with an automatic rifle. Ten police cars and a helicopter were summoned to track the dangerous, evil gunman – whose weapon turned out to be a giant salami.

He started up his mechanical digger, approached his colleague and accidentally sliced off his head.

A Dutchman who has had the appalling luck to have lost both of his legs in separate accidents is not happy with the Dutch Health Service's latest attempt to help him in his plight. Jelle Wagt lost his right leg in 1998 after a fall into the hold of a ship, and was given a false leg. So far, so good, except that that right leg was a little too long. Then, recently, Mr Wagt had his left leg amputated after another accident, and on his recovery was sent home with another false leg, which he didn't try on until he got home, only to discover that it, too, was a right leg. Mr Wagt said that walking with

STRANGE

In Holland, a man called the police and the fire brigade to alert them to a house fire after he saw flames sprouting from the roof of a neighbour's house in the town of Duiven. Firefighters arrived to find absolutely no fire at all, and were just about to get extremely stroppy with the man who called them out when one of the firemen noticed that the reflection of the sun's rays on water in the house's gutter looked just like flames, making it look as though the house was indeed on fire.

two right feet just didn't feel comfortable. At least he didn't end up with two left feet.

A Taiwanese school received a grant of about $300,000 to turn a small wetland on the school grounds into a special ecology park as a habitat for butterflies. The wetland had been a source of local pride for about thirty years, but when water authorities checked the pipes in the area, it turned out that it was caused by a leak. Now the 'wetland' has dried up, but on the upside, at least the school's water bill has dropped by 80 per cent!

A farmer in Wisconsin placed a cast-iron cow in his field to scare off birds. What he didn't anticipate, though, was the inflammatory effect the cow scarecrow would have on the local bull population, 50 of whom suffered groin injuries as they tried to give it a good seeing-to. The farmer was sued for vets' bills by several local dairy farmers.

A Dutch cinema owner ordered a film for a group of elderly farmers' wives that he thought they would enjoy: Roman Polanski's Academy Award-winning *The Pianist*. But the group, which rents out Dirk Holeman's cinema once a month, were treated to *La Pianiste*, about a woman addicted to pornography and sadistic sex. The chairwoman of the group said that no harm had been done, and that they were amused to see men 'holding on for such a long time'. (That was probably a cinematic trick, ladies.) Holeman vowed to get the right film, though, and offered free tickets to the ladies.

There was a tiny, insignificant little oversight in the city of Newcastle when a £5 million library was built. The city council completely forgot to order any books, or even shelves to put them on.

And staying with the naughty film theme, a vicar gave his flock hardcore porn videos instead of a video about God's message at Christmas after a mix-up at a copying factory. About 300 churchgoers ended up with the triple-X-rated material in the German village of Lampoldshausen. Local parish priest Frithjof Schwesig estimated that only five to seven people in the village actually watched the film. As Father Frithjof pointed out, God moves in mysterious ways, and the people who were expecting porn had religious films about Jesus in their video recorders. Whether this made them religious or furious is anyone's guess.

An Italian family got a rude awakening when they discovered that after fifteen years of visiting a cemetery to pay their respects to a dead relative, they had been praying at the wrong grave. The tombstone on the grave they were visiting had been mixed up

Romania's president, Ion Iliescu, lunched at the Pentagon in Washington DC with the US Defence Secretary, Donald Rumsfeld. Guess which flag the table was decorated with. The Romanian flag? Of course not – that would be too obvious. No, when the leader ate at the Pentagon, there was the Russian flag on the table.

with the one next to it. Local authorities apologised and offered a 'free grave plot' to the family as compensation.

Sometimes you take things for granted. A women's prison would assume that any prisoner arriving to serve a sentence would be a woman. Even so, as in the case of Kentucky's Correctional Institute for Women, a strip search is usually carried out on the inmate before they are admitted. Which is why it came as something of a shock when Billie Jo Hawks told warders, after spending eight months inside the prison, that he was a man, not a woman. And it was only the prospect of a medical examination that made him own up. The 43-year-old (yes, 43 – not some young androgynous thing) had somehow already spent eight months in the women's section of a detention centre before being transferred to the prison.

Prince Charles probably meant well, but his intended act of kindness was a potential act of cruelty. As a 'get well' gesture he sent a present to heavy rocker Ozzy Osbourne, in hospital after a quad bike accident, and well known (to everyone except finger-on-the-pulse Prince Charles) as a recovering alcoholic. The present? A bottle of whisky.

Britain's most popular hillwalking magazine *Trail* regularly includes route maps for stimulating and challenging walks. But it was forced to apologise for a regrettable error in one issue last year. It contained a route that led climbers straight off the sheer edge of Ben Nevis's notorious north face.

sorry, what did you say?

A Dorset man, Ieuan Llewellyn, was on holiday in Mexico and volunteered for a soccer kickabout in a bullring, along with five other tourists. All five were given helmets, oddly, and as the five entered the arena in front of 1,500 spectators, the compere whispered to him, 'Watch out for the ball.' Or so Ieuan thought. What he actually said was 'Watch out for the bull.' And Ieuan was gored nine times by the furious bull as it charged into the ring.

MONEY TO BURN

Every year people set fire to money, probably to remind us that there are more important things in life ...

A postal worker in Argentina burned what he thought was nothing more than a pile of old paper while he was cleaning a post office in the town of Tucuman. But it was the post office's takings for the week, totalling about £3,000. A post office spokesperson said: 'The cleaner is very distressed, but he will have to replace that money.'

FORGETFULNESS

We like artificial limb stories here at *Another Weird Year*: managers at Water World, a swimming leisure complex in Stoke-on-Trent, had their annual clearout of lost property last year and were dumbfounded to see that in the cupboard were no fewer than ten artificial arms and legs, absent-mindedly left in the changing rooms by their owners. How someone could turn up for a swim with four limbs and go home with three beggars belief. This almost proves that some people would forget their own heads if they weren't screwed on. All the limbs were subsequently recovered by their owners.

Plain Stupid

From the toolbox that is the world, we present the blunter ones, those with incomplete pizzas, and whose lifts don't quite go up to the top floor.

The ideas you get into your head. And the stupid ideas stupid people get into their heads. A woman in the US state of Louisiana had somehow got it into her head that you couldn't be arrested in the safety of your own home. And after she was arrested, in the safety of her own driveway, having led police on a high-speed car chase, she said that she knew this because she had seen it on a TV show.

A man in Perth, Western Australia, noticed that the battery of his mobile phone was running low. So he decided to recharge it – in his microwave oven. The battery exploded and firefighters had to be called to deal with the flames. The man escaped unharmed, and we await his next moronic act with interest.

STUPID

Police had noticed her driving without a licence plate and tried to pull her over, but she just speeded up and joined a motorway, driving madly at 95 mph while cars from three other police forces joined the chase. She drove to her home town of Alexandria, pulled up the driveway and walked towards her house as if nothing had happened, before they grabbed her.

A Croatian woman in Germany was due to go on holiday with her boyfriend, but as the departure day grew closer she became more and more uncertain about it. She was scared of telling her parents she was going away with a man, and just as scared of telling her boyfriend her parents didn't approve. So she took the most obvious course of action to get out of her quandary: she phoned Düsseldorf airport, where they were due to fly from, claiming to be an Al Qaeda

Stupid act number 1: when a man parked his car in a sloping car park in Portsmouth to go and walk his dog, he didn't secure the hand-brake. Stupid act number 2: as the Nissan Primera hurtled down the hill towards him, he tried to stop it by standing in front of it. He was killed by his own car.

terrorist, causing authorities to shut down the whole airport, stranding 64,000 passengers and instigating a mass police search for a bomb. Well, what would *you* have done?

In the last edition of *Another Weird Year* we had a Swede using a vacuum cleaner on a parking meter. Now here's a German, from Frankfurt, using a vacuum cleaner on his car, but in the stupidest possible way. He mistakenly refuelled his car, a diesel, with petrol. Could happen to anyone. Then, after siphoning the petrol out of the tank with the help of the forecourt attendant, he decided to make sure the tank was totally empty. He took the nozzle of the vacuum cleaner provided on the forecourt and stuck it into the fuel tank. There were, of course, a few drops of petrol in the tank, they were sucked into the cleaner where the heat ignited them and caused the cleaner to explode, causing about £1,000 of damage.

A Canadian woman very stupidly set off a totally needless terrorist alert in the city of Edmonton. She rang the emergency services to report that the paper of a letter she had just received had suddenly changed from white to pale yellow, and then darkened to brown. A sinister chemical attack on an unsuspecting easy target? Chemical hazard officers arrived at the scene and were able to reassure the woman that she had put the letter down in a small pool of spilled coffee.

stagestruck and stupid

These days in the UK reality TV is big business, and it seems more and more people are fired up about it and the fact that it can turn any old knobhead into a star. One of the biggest dailies, the *Daily Mirror*, decided to test just how stupidly low the general public would go in their desire to appear on a reality TV show. They put out ads for a spoof reality show, Quarantine, asking for contestants willing to spend a week in a lab exposed to revolting infectious diseases, in return for the instant fame of being on camera twenty-four hours a day. They received 200 applications.

Also in Canada, a student celebrated his 20th birthday by trying so hard to win a spitting contest taking place on an eleventh-floor balcony that he fell over the railing and plunged to his death. Lots of booze and an overlong run-up to his spit attempt, plus a fair amount of stupidity, were to blame.

Medical ignorance is forgivable – we can't all be experts. But a little basic knowledge does help sometimes. In a Rio de Janeiro clinic a man suffering from an ear infection was mistakenly called to the surgery of a doctor whose next patient was up for a vasectomy. The man underwent the vasectomy without a murmur because he thought his ear problem must have had deeper roots than usual.

More medical idiocy: in Melbourne, Australia, an obese woman went to hospital, telling doctors she was pregnant, and suffered a heart attack. Surgeons immediately performed a Caesarean on her to deliver the baby, just in case her heart attack proved fatal, only to find that she had been lying and there was no baby. The woman survived.

A BIT DIM

An Indian man set an unusual record last year. At the age of 18 Shivdan Yadav put off his marriage to a girl in his village until he had passed his school exams, vowing not to marry her until he had them under his belt. First time round, he failed them, but the bride's family, who admired his studious attitude, were happy to postpone the wedding again. Three years and three sets of failed exams went by, and his bride's family found her another young man. At that stage Mr Yadav promised not to marry until he had passed those damn exams, but at the age of 56 he set a record for having taken them 38 times. Failed every time for 38 years. Too dim to pass, too dim to stop trying. Who'd marry *him*?

FEEDING THE FLAMES OF STUPIDITY

What are the odds on this? Not one, not two but three stories that share the theme of stupid people burning down their houses trying to deal with vermin.

Ranvir Singh, of the Indian village of Nagla Plal, caught a mouse in a trap. Clever. Well, done, Ranvir. Then he decided to kill it; not with a sharp blow to the head, for example, but in a way that almost defies belief. He dipped a cloth in kerosene, tied it to the mouse's tail and lit it, intending to burn the mouse to death. Just as the cloth burst into flames, the mouse escaped and ran round Ranvir's house, setting fire to objects as it passed, until the whole house was ablaze.

A Swiss man discovered a wasps' nest underneath an overhanging roof outside his apartment in Zurich and went for the overkill approach, emptying an entire aerosol spraycan of insect repellent into it. Unsurprisingly, the wasps streamed out of the nest and the man lit his cigarette lighter to scare them away from him. Equally unsurprisingly, the lighter flame ignited the insect spray and set the apartment on fire, the flames spreading rapidly so that not only was his apartment burned down but also two others.

And in an incident that proves that using fire to deal with pests is definitely extremely unwise, Rogerio Assis Cavalcante, a Brazilian, also lost his house to flames when he lit a sheet of paper to disperse a swarm of mosquitoes that had flown into his house. The flames spread like ... like wildfire, really, and very soon it was time to call the fire brigade.

Not a vermin attack in this story, but a similar end result. A Moscow man went from having dirty trousers and an apartment to having no trousers, no washing machine and a wrecked apartment. He decided that a good way to get rid of stubborn paint stains on a pair of trousers would be to add a litre of petrol to his washing machine. But guess what – it caused a huge explosion that blew up the washing machine, destroyed the kitchen and brought down two of the apartment's internal walls.

ABUSING THE EMERGENCY SERVICES

People – stupid people, that is – are becoming less and less clear on what constitutes an emergency. So when in doubt, they dial that special number ...

Lula Brown, of Ohio, called the emergency services to complain that the McDonald's she was eating in had tried to charge her for an extra helping of barbecue sauce. The police eventually decided not to arrest her for '911 abuse'.

Now let's not be too hard on Lizka Litton when she dialled 999 from her home in Coventry to say that she was vomiting blood – she was genuinely ill and in a lot of pain. Ms Litton had been waiting seven months for an operation on a severe case of hiatus hernia and was worried that waiting longer would push her close to death's door. So when the ambulance men arrived, what they were shown in a container was not freshly vomited blood but a blend of cranberry juice and crumbled biscuits. It fooled the ambulance men, though, and she was taken to hospital, having cunningly disposed of the 'blood' so that doctors could not foil her plan, and had her operation.

SHIRKING RESPONSIBILITY

If you ignore the problem, it'll just go away. Won't it?

Chicago police detective Janice Govern was doing a bit of peaceful shopping in a Dominick's food store when a customer told her that the store's bank branch was being held up. She must have momentarily

A German man, normally a reliable member of his decorating firm in Koblenz, didn't turn up to work one day and eventually his employers called the police when there was no answer to their telephone calls. The police forced their way into his house and found the man sitting in his wardrobe. He said he just wanted some peace and quiet.

ECCENTRIC

forgotten what she did for a living, because she told the customer to dial 911, and then got on with her shopping. When officers arrived to investigate the crime, she was still in the store, waiting to pay for her shopping. Govern was put up for dismissal from the force.

A man lay dead for two days at the foot of the stairs at home, while his family stepped over him to get up and down stairs. Gareth Duggan's dad and brother thought that he was playing a practical joke and never tried to rouse him. They even threw a blanket over him to keep him warm. It was thought that 24-year-old Duggan died after drinking in his room in Neath, south Wales. Giving his verdict on the death, Coroner David Osbourne said drug user Duggan could be an aloof person, but added that 46 hours was stretching the limits for a wind-up.

Nutty as a Fruitcake

A man from north-western Turkey, who, at the age of 53, had never eaten sweets, suddenly decided he wanted to see what he had been missing all his life. So, to get back up to speed on the sugar-consumption front, he ate 15 kg (33 lb) of honey over a ten-day period. On the tenth day Hayri Ates went into a coma, with blood sugar levels of 760 mg, and it took him another day before he returned to consciousness. Older, wiser, and considerably sweeter, he promised to keep his sugar intake at more reasonable levels.

A 48-year-old German woman developed heart problems after consuming nearly a pound of liquorice a day for four months. Her massive binge came to an abrupt end when she collapsed, and then was unable to work for several months. And in accordance with these uncontrollably litigious times, she tried to sue the sweets company Haribo for €6,000 for fuelling her addiction.

WEIRD

Police in Pasadena, Texas, were looking for a man with a very strange approach to paying visits on people. Reports were given to the police of a masked man dressed in black and carrying a Barbie doll. He knocked on a woman's door and carried on knocking after the door was opened, waving the Barbie doll, and saying nothing. A neighbour in the same apartment block also heard a knock and saw a man waving a Barbie doll in front of her peephole.

And if you think a masked man dressed in black and carrying a Barbie doll is weird, what about William Rhode of the US state of New Jersey? Rhode

A story that popped up last year concerned an Indian taxi driver and his wife, who became the object of attention because they were in the habit of driving everywhere backwards. Harpreet Devi, from Bhatinda, started driving that way when his car got stuck in reverse gear one day, he was unable to release it and he was forced to drive 35 miles home. That incident, he said, made him realise that he could drive anywhere and everywhere backwards, and he and his wife Krishna motor along in traffic at up to 25 mph.

was arrested after visiting several daycare centres and a school, asking for employment. His visits didn't go unnoticed – he was wearing pink women's tights and a very large nappy. And when he was at the Holy Spirit School he relieved himself into the nappy in front of the pupils.

Now cycling is a wonderful, wonderful thing, and a love of bikes is something to be encouraged. But it would seem that someone encouraged a man in the Australian town of Geelong, near Melbourne, a little too much. When the 60-year-old man died while trying to steal a bike in Melbourne, police eventually found their way to his home, where they were astonished to find around 1,000 bicycles of all shapes, styles and sizes. It was hard to establish how many he had stolen, since he was also known to like buying bikes. It took police four hours and two truckloads just to remove the first 100 bikes from his house.

The obsessive you'd most want to steal your car (except he never stole private cars, only cars from garage showrooms) was sent to prison when his bizarre car-stealing past caught up with him. Colin Sadd (described as 'aptly named' by one judge) would dress in a smart suit and tie and pose as a customer at car showrooms throughout Yorkshire, dazzling the sales-men with his phenomenal knowledge of car types and specifications. Requesting a test drive, he would snatch the keys and zoom off, driving around for several hours before washing the car, polishing it and thoroughly cleaning the interior. Then he would leave the gleaming, carefully valeted car for the owners to reclaim. Sadd's wife Mary said after his sentence that she was ending their 13-year marriage, pointing out that, 'He looked after the cars he stole better than me. I can't even afford to file for divorce.'

A certain Roger Chamberlain checked out of a motel in New York State, and cleaning staff went into his room, to discover that every surface in the room had been covered with Vaseline. Mattresses, bedding, the TV, the armchair, all covered in petroleum jelly. The carpets, the towels, the curtains ... all liberally smeared with the stuff. The rubbish bin contained 14 empty jars of Vaseline, as well as some porn mags. Damage to the room was estimated at about $1,000, and the sheriff was called to trace the mysterious and very slippery Mr Chamberlain. Unable to give them the slip, he was tracked down at another motel, not far away, apparently 'smeared from head to foot with Vaseline'.

The Red Mist

Anger is one of the seven deadly sins, and the one most likely to harm others. Or objects. Anger is when the individual 'spurns love and opts instead for fury'. Don't give in to it. Count to ten, or twenty. These people didn't ...

One gloomy winter's day in Norway, a man became so enraged with his son that he did damage that he would one day live to regret. Except at the time he didn't regret it. The son's BMW happened to break down at the entrance to a car park in the town of Buskerud, and by chance his father, a snow clearer by profession, arrived there at the same time in a mechanical snow shoveller, to clear the car park. They started talking, but an old argument reappeared, and the red mist began to rise into the father's brain. As his son sat in his BMW, the father used his shoveller to heap snow in high walls around it. His son got out and climbed into his father's vehicle to carry on the angry argument, then smashed the window of the shoveller.

Not to be outdone, the father simply winched up the shovel and brought it down onto the roof of the BMW, totally crushing it. Neither man was hurt, but the police had to be called to calm things down.

How angry is it possible to get? In a block of flats in the American town of Ridgefield, a woman was getting angry about the noise coming from the flat below hers. The music that Allen Haines was playing annoyed Toni Lynn Lacan, so she jumped up and down on the floor by way of complaint. That didn't bother her neighbour – he just turned up the volume. Even more enraged, Lacan jumped up and down even harder, bringing her legs down so hard that she broke both legs just below the knee.

The intention was beyond reproach: the ninth grade of Woodlawn High School, in the US city of Baltimore, were assembled for a workshop on anger management. As students on stage role-played peaceful ways of resolving conflict, parents and students in the main group dealt with conflict in the short-term way – with violence. As a parent confronted a group she believed had bullied her child, a shoving match ensued, which degenerated into a mass ruck of 750 students. The police had to be called to quell the mob, and there were two arrests, as well as 11 suspensions.

One thing that really riles me is having my precious sleep disturbed. I don't have a gun, but a Spanish man had ... The 60-year-old man, in Barcelona, shot dead two street musicians who kept him awake at night playing on the street below his apartment. The two men, who were from Portugal, had been playing an electric organ in their delivery truck and drinking beer. One was hit in the head and died instantly, and the other died later in hospital.

Fergus Glen, 36, from Wainuiomata, New Zealand, killed his younger brother Craig by hacking him to death with an axe. The reason for his murderous rage? Craig had not thanked him for cooking dinner.

st valentine's day massacre

Hell hath no fury like a mad boyfriend scorned on St Valentine's Day. In New York City, Betsaida Eva Madera refused the marriage proposal of her boyfriend, Wilfred Lopez. Shortly afterwards she was found dead in her apartment, her throat slashed and a gaping hole in her chest where Lopez had cut out her heart.

Two women got quite angry with each other – boyfriend stuff – at a party in Bridgeport, in the US state of Connecticut, and the argument escalated into a fight. Woman A had turned up at the party with the boyfriend of Woman B, to which Woman B objected. But Woman A was so enraged by the argument that she took her opponent's hand and bit off one of the fingers. The fight was broken up, but to make things even worse, someone flushed the finger down the toilet.

AN ASSORTMENT OF RAGES

Spam rage

A Silicon Valley computer programmer succumbed to spam rage after an unending barrage of junk email ads promising to enlarge his penis, and threatened to torture and kill employees of the company he thought was responsible for the ads. Charles Booher, 44, from Sunnyvale, California, threatened to send a package full of anthrax spores to the company, to 'disable' an employee with a bullet and torture him with a power drill and ice pick; and to hunt down and castrate the employees unless they removed him from their email list, prosecutors said at his trial. The object of the Californian's anger was Douglas Mackay, president of DM Contact Management, which works for Albion Medical, a firm advertising the 'Only Reliable, Medically

pump rage

A Florida woman was refused alcohol at a filling station because according to state law alcohol cannot be sold before 6 a.m. Debra Marren screamed and bawled at the sales assistant, but he stuck to his guns, and she went back to her car, revved it up and drove it straight into a petrol pump, which promptly exploded.

ODD

Approved Penis Enhancement'. He said his firm does not send spam but blamed a rival firm which he said routes much of their unsolicited bulk email through Russia and Eastern Europe. Mackay said firms like those gave a bad name to the penis enhancement business.

Pampering rage

Lamar McGranthin, of Newport Township in the US state of Pennsylvania, got so angry with his neighbour, Sharon Pezzuti, that he had her convicted of criminal trespass. Her crime? Sneaking into his garden and pampering his Alsatian dog, Blue. Ms Pezzuti bought Blue a kennel and an automatic dog feeder, and even whisked him away one night to take him to the vet when she thought he wasn't well. (Her defence was that Blue was being neglected.)

Mayo rage

Deep in the heart of Texas, a woman got very, very angry. Waynetta Nolan was sentenced to 10 years in prison after a bout of mayonnaise rage led her to run over the manager of a McDonald's with her car. First, when Nolan asked for mayo on her cheeseburger at the drive-through window and was refused, she threw the burger at the window. To calm her down, the manager then offered Nolan a fresh cheeseburger, with mayo, but Nolan was already scenting blood, and began to make a series of random food demands, until the manager came out to note down her number plate. At this point Nolan simply ran her down, breaking her pelvis. (She claimed it was an accident due to her putting ketchup on her burger while pulling away.)

christmas lights rage

At an apartment complex in Florida the residents got into the community spirit of Christmas by having a competition to see who had the most attractive display. The winner was announced – one Donna Simmons-Groover – and a neighbour was immediately stricken with Christmas lights rage, ripping down part of her more beautiful display and unplugging some of her cables. He thought he should have won.

Snowball rage

A German magistrate, in the town of Dahlenburg, decided to shout at two teenagers who were throwing snowballs at his house; just as he opened the window a snowball hit him in the face. Given the option of turning the other cheek and staying calm, or exploding with rage, reaching for his double-barrelled shotgun and shooting at the two boys, he went for the course of action that got him arrested. He shot one of the 16-year-olds in the arm, and was later arrested for attempted manslaughter.

Artificial leg rage

An American man in Fredericksburg, Virginia, was arrested after succumbing to artificial limb rage. Michael Clapp, owner of the leg in question, noticed that a bottle of medicine was missing from his flat, and confronted his neighbour, Rodney Prophitt, who he was sure had stolen it. Prophitt was so infuriated by the accusation that he pushed Clapp over, removed his artificial leg and beat him with it. Clapp was treated in hospital for a broken nose and other facial injuries, while police charged Prophitt with assault and theft.

Cinema rage

Sometimes a place of culture and spiritual elevation, sometimes a place of anger – it all depends on the movie, or even the audience. At a US showing of the

tyre rage

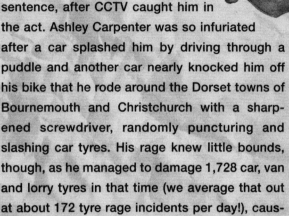

A ten-day tyre-slashing spree cost a rage-ridden cyclist a prison sentence, after CCTV caught him in the act. Ashley Carpenter was so infuriated after a car splashed him by driving through a puddle and another car nearly knocked him off his bike that he rode around the Dorset towns of Bournemouth and Christchurch with a sharpened screwdriver, randomly puncturing and slashing car tyres. His rage knew little bounds, though, as he managed to damage 1,728 car, van and lorry tyres in that time (we average that out at about 172 tyre rage incidents per day!), causing a total of £250,000 of damage. And a lot of immobilised cars and stranded drivers.

gentle comedy animation *Belleville Rendezvous*, things got violent when one member of the audience shushed another whose constant chatting was proving a distraction and an annoyance. It was a shush too far, though, as the shushee erupted into rage, punching the shusher in the face and pushing him down the stairs. Result: broken ribs for the shusher and arrest for GBH for the shushee.

LUCK

AIRBORNE LUCK

Sixty-seven-year-old Dorothy Fletcher was on a flight from the UK to Orlando, in Florida, for her daughter's wedding. Her bad luck was to suffer a heart attack during the flight. When the flight attendant put out the traditional 'Is there a doctor on the plane?' call, Mrs Fletcher's bad luck turned to good as 15 cardiologists stood up and rushed to her rescue. They were on their way to a cardiology conference in Orlando.

Louis Kadlecek, 21, broke into an aircraft hangar at an airport near Lake Jackson, Texas, and climbed aboard a Cessna 172. The thing was, Kadlecek had never even been in an aeroplane before, but by trial and error – and a small slice of luck – he managed to get the plane started and then airborne. Aiming to fly to Mexico, he covered about one mile before crashing into power lines. The aeroplane plummeted to the ground, and was completely wrecked. Kadlecek's larger slice of luck was walking away from the crash without any injury.

GREAT ESCAPES

In an incident that a Hollywood film crew would have had difficulty staging so perfectly, a car fell out of a multi-storey car park and landed next to a man walking along the street. It happened in the Australian town of Dapto, near Sydney, and came about when a driver missed a turn inside the car park and went straight down a ramp into a parked car, sending it shooting over the barrier and launching it into the air. The man, Adam Bardon, suffered a few injuries from the barrier itself and shattered glass, but avoided being squashed flat by mere inches.

An accident-induced Heimlich manoeuvre saved the life of a driver in the US state of North Carolina. Eddie May Jr was eating while driving on a busy Interstate Highway, and began choking on a piece of food. He became dizzy, then blacked out completely. May's pick-up truck then veered suddenly across onto the other carriageway and hit an articulated lorry a glancing blow. The collision caused the offending morsel of food to jump out from his windpipe, May breathed a deep lungful of air and swiftly regained consciousness – to find that his truck was a total wreck. And to add to May's good luck index on that day, despite not wearing a seat belt, he walked away from the crash unharmed, the other driver was also unharmed, and despite having swerved across several lanes of lunchtime rush-hour traffic, May had caused no other accidents. He was done for dangerous driving and not wearing a seat belt, though.

A gruesome and grim accident had a happy ending in Germany, when a building worker, Harry Moeller, was drilling foundations on a building site near Munich. The soft ground he was attacking with his pneumatic drill caused the drill to somersault in his hands. The drill bit – a foot long – immediately pierced his neck. Harry's wife Karin arrived moments later with his lunch, to find him on the ground with the drill, still running, in his neck. In hospital, after Moeller had been airlifted there by helicopter, still conscious and asking

Henry Kuttner cheated death after a visit to his public library, in north London, turned into a nightmare. Mr Kuttner's heart pacemaker was reset by the library's electronic security gates, and his heart started beating at a near fatal frequency. A few days in hospital, well away from the mantrap of the library, sorted him out. We hope he hasn't still got books that need returning, though.

when he'd be able to drink beer again, surgeons found that the drill had missed major blood vessels and nerves by a centimetre.

Eighteen-year-old Ben Brown of Newbury had been out drinking with a friend, missed his train home and decided to walk home along the track. He was hit by a train travelling at 110 mph, thrown to the side of the track and lay there for six hours before a nearby resident heard his screams and called the

This last year an American man made history by becoming the first person to survive going over Niagara Falls without any buoyancy aid or protective apparatus. Even with floats, padding and the like, the Niagara Falls experience tends to be fatal. Kirk Jones, from Michigan, dressed in normal clothes and a parka jacket, climbed over the iron fence on the Canadian side of the Falls, made his way down to some rocks by the side of the rushing water and simply stepped in, in full view of the regular tourist crowds. He was immediately swept over the 55-metre drop into the rock-filled gorge below. Four minutes elapsed with no sign of him; then Jones emerged, swam to shore and walked away with nothing more than bruised ribs.

BIZARRE

police. Ben suffered nothing more than a broken wrist and injuries to his ankles and left knee, and made a full recovery. How he was not killed outright by a train travelling at such a speed no one will ever know.

Four-year-old Livia Ungureanu plunged from a third-floor balcony at her home in the Romanian town of Baile Olanesti. Had she landed on the pavement she would undoubtedly have died, but since she landed on a stray dog, she was fine, sustaining only minor injuries. Livia had been throwing food over the balcony to the dog when she leaned too far and overbalanced, so it was only right that the dog should save the life of its benefactor. And what goes around comes around – the dog got lucky too, when Livia's grandma agreed that the dog, which was also not badly hurt, could be adopted as a pet.

HANGING IN THERE

A 40-year spell of bad luck mixed with amazing escapes was laid to rest in the most satisfying way possible for Croatian music teacher Frane Selak. Starting in 1962, Selak has suffered blow after blow, escaping with his life on many occasions. First he was on a train that derailed on a river bridge in winter, plunging into the frigid water below, a disaster that took the lives of 17 people; in 1963 he and many others were sucked out of a DC-8 aeroplane when a door suddenly

amazing coincidence

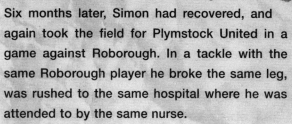

In March 2003, Simon May of Devon broke his leg playing football for Plymstock United against Roborough.

Six months later, Simon had recovered, and again took the field for Plymstock United in a game against Roborough. In a tackle with the same Roborough player he broke the same leg, was rushed to the same hospital where he was attended to by the same nurse.

opened – 18 died, but he landed in a haystack. In 1966 he was in a bus that crashed into a river, resulting in four deaths – Salek made it to the shore. His unlucky/lucky incidents stayed with transport but moved to cars: in 1970 his car burst into flames as he drove on a motorway, and he freed himself seconds before the fuel tank blew up. And three years later as he drove along, the car's fuel pump leaked petrol onto the engine, which ignited and was sucked into the car through the air vents, setting fire to Salek's hair. More recently he was knocked down by a city bus in Zagreb, and drove his car off the side of a mountain, leaping free and landing in a tree before it exploded lower down. Add four failed marriages to the mix, and you can see why he was so jubilant when, with his first lottery ticket for 40 years, he won the £600,000 jackpot.

BAD LUCK

Ornithologists noted with delight that a wren, a tiny bird not given to long migratory journeys, had made the first ever recorded flight from Norway to Britain. Delight turned to sorrow as it turned out that this brave little creature, weighing no more than a £1 coin, had ended its epic 310-mile voyage by landing in a pot of glue on an oil rig, where it died.

Birdwatchers in the UK knew both pleasure and pain when an American robin, thousands of miles off course from its migratory path, nested on an industrial site in Grimsby. This incredibly rare sighting – only a dozen have ever been seen in Britain – was brought to a bloody and premature end when, in full view of all the twitchers, a sparrowhawk swooped upon the poor robin and devoured it.

Another bird mishap, for an extremely rare feathered visitor to Britain. In the last century, only 30 Scandinavian robins have been known to arrive in Britain. When one does, birdwatchers are cock-a-hoop – apart from the birdwatcher who realised that a Scandinavian robin had survived the 15-hour, 400-mile flight from Norway because it ended up in her back garden in Manchester. Unfortunately the reason she saw it so clearly was that it was in the death grip of her own cat's jaws.

Wearing your door key on a cord around your neck is a sure-fire way of not losing it. What you might lose, though, is your life, if you're as unlucky as Kieran Duggal of south-west London. As Duggal leaned forward to unlock his front door he slipped, got the cord tangled round his neck and throttled himself.

When Englishman Jim Hughes set sail for a round-the-world voyage in 2002, his attempt foundered when Icelandic fisherman Eriker Olafsson crashed into his luxury yacht off the south coast of England, causing £25,000 worth of damage. A year later, Hughes was ready to go again, and moored in the same place. Olafsson spotted Hughes's yacht and sailed over in his own vessel to apologise for wrecking his boat the year before, and crashed into it again, causing £18,000 worth of damage. Olafsson then tried to untangle the boats, failed and tried to get away, dragging Hughes's yacht for five miles from its moorings and once again ruining his chances of his global voyage.

A catalogue of bad luck for one Tom Jones of Dorset. The 84-year-old got his bed wet after stepping out of the shower and sitting on it. So he tried to dry it with a hairdryer. But that set the mattress on fire. So he dragged the burning mattress out of the house and onto the front porch. But that somehow caused a gas pipe to catch fire, and the flames quickly reached

A factory owner in Thailand went to see a fortune-teller for advice about his financial problems. The fortune-teller gave him a flag that was supposed to have magical powers and told the 43-year-old businessman to fly it from the roof of his factory to ward off bad luck. As the man was on the roof of his factory trying to put up the flag, he slipped and fell to his death.

the roof. As fears of a massive gas explosion grew, four neighbouring families were evacuated as fire crews and gas engineers arrived. The road had to be dug up to cut off the gas supply. Tom Jones went to stay with relatives after all that, while some wit pointed out that his namesake, Tom Jones the singer, once had a hit with 'Burning Down the House'.

Lightning never strikes twice in the same place, they say, so if you've been struck once and stay still, you ought to be safe. Not in the case of Ryan Sayers, out climbing in the Rocky Mountains. He and his girlfriend were hit by lightning while ascending Steeple Peak, and survived. They decided to stay put and sit out the storm, but an hour later a second strike hit Sayers – this time he didn't survive.

Anthony Askew of Pembrokeshire was doing a spot of decorating at home when he slipped off his ladder and fell to the floor. Unfortunately, his 15-month-old son had just toddled into the room and took the full force of his father's body, dying from the impact.

GOOD AND BAD LUCK

So, the good luck: Carl Atwood won $57,000 on a televised lottery show in the US state of Indiana. He went straight home from the studio, after the programme was taped, to his home town with his cheque safely in his pocket, and went over to the grocery store where he bought the lottery ticket. The bad luck: as he crossed the road he was hit by a pick-up truck and later died. At least the family will have plenty of money to pay for a really nice funeral.

The good luck: Peter Dickinson, of Lancashire, found a liver donor and had his diseased liver replaced successfully in an operation that surgeons said would add ten years to his life. The bad luck: the donor, unknown to anyone, had cancer, and Dickinson's new liver passed the cancer on to him, causing his death just 11 months later.

A small Polish port hit the news last year when it decided to give its patron a makeover to attract more tourists to the town, called Ustka, on the Baltic coast. The patron in question is a statue of a mermaid, and the town councillors decided that if she had larger breasts and a slimmer waist this would be a boon for the town's rather somnolent tourist industry. The debate itself certainly attracted attention, but it remains to be seen whether a foxier mermaid pulls in the punters.

Lena Skarning was awarded a nice business start-up grant from her government. No reason why not – she had put together a sound business plan which her local development office in Nord Odal and Hedmark, Norway, described as 'well thought out'. Ms Skarning's business success makes her Norway's only state-sponsored witch. Her company, Forest Witch Magic Consulting, will tell fortunes, teach magic tricks at corporate seminars, and offer potions and creams to deal with problems such as sleeplessness and bad habits. Skarning's grant has a condition attached to it,

When times are hard in public finance, cuts to yodellers' lederhosen subsidies just have to be made. The government of the German state of Bavaria announced that it could no longer afford state aid, previously amounting to 500,000 euros, to help its yodellers buy lederhosen. 'We no longer want to sponsor the lederhosen with subsidies,' Bavarian Premier Edmund Stoiber said, despite outrage from traditional folk groups with total membership of around 300,000, some of whom threatened to boycott the opening parade of the Munich Oktoberfest, the world's biggest beer festival. A good pair of goat suede leather lederhosen costs about 150 euros.

though: she must not use her spells to harm anyone. No problem – Skarning, 33, has been a 'nice witch' for her whole career. Nice, and also very business-savvy.

Here's what you get for thirty years' dedication: American Chuck Strickler worked for thirty years as a welder at various US nuclear power stations, the result of which was that his fingerprints were almost completely worn away. US nuclear plants started insisting on using fingerprints as identification for all employees, so poor old Chuck got the boot.

You've heard about fat cats creaming off the money from big businesses, awarding themselves huge salaries, but this is more than a fat cat – a clinically obese feline, maybe. It emerged at the trial in the US of John Rigas, founder of Adelphia Communications, that he owned 22 luxury cars, all paid for by the company and that, even more extravagantly, he was taking out so much cash during the 1990s that his son, a company executive, was forced to limit him to $1 million a month.

Proof, if proof were needed, that the advertising industry runs a bit low on morals now and then: a Czech radio station that has as its slogan 'Radio For Life' used the image of a lifer – a murderer serving a life

clever business

Is this a story of brilliant salesmanship or a sad indictment of the extent of consumerism? You decide. December in New York City, and a blizzard swept over the Big Apple. As New Yorkers gambolled (probably having first called their therapists to check that it was OK to play) in the snow, Gilberto Triplett set up a little street-corner stall selling ... snowballs. $1 each. Stock started at six fresh snowballs, which he shifted straight away; he restocked and sold four more before walking away.

STRANGE

sentence – on billboards promoting Radio Kiss. Jiri Kajinek, 43, was in line to earn thousands of pounds for his appearance in the ad campaign, to add to his notoriety as one of the Czech Republic's most feared criminals – he murdered a businessman and his bodyguard, then escaped from a top security prison, staying on the run for six weeks. Radio Kiss director Jan Cadek said he hoped using the murderer's image would 'stimulate debate'.

SOMEONE'S GOT TO DO IT

Norwegian teenager Svein Tore Hauge landed himself a great summer job. Working at the Saerheim Plant Research centre, his job was to follow cows in the fields, catching their dung as it came out. In order for it to be useful for scientific study, the excreta has to be free of grass and mud, so Svein had to make sure he got good and close and caught it in mid-flow. As he said, 'Sometimes, it's easy, but sometimes it just sprays in all directions.'

The Milwaukee Metropolitan Sewerage District revealed, when it was making a request for more funding, that it was paying a man about $460 a day to scoop used condoms from the chlorine tanks at its Jones Island plant.

PAYMENT IN KIND

In the last edition of *Another Weird Year* we noted a payment in prawns and coffins instead of cash; and people are still brightening up the dull world of trade with non-monetary deals.

Alan and Gloria Reynolds of Gloucestershire were anxious to part-exchange their old Ford Ka for a £6,000 Fiat Punto, but were offered only £2,000 for their Ford Ka. Since their budget stopped at the £3,500 mark, they were £500 short of their new motor, and the salesman wasn't budging an inch. As a last-gasp deal-clincher, Alan put Charlie into the deal. Charlie is a Mealy Amazon parrot, and his price was £500. The salesman went to his manager and came back with good news: the Punto was theirs for the Ford Ka, £3,500 and an Amazon parrot. Charlie now sits in his cage at Sanderson Motorhouse in Cheltenham, whistling at customers and doing impressions of the fax machine.

The management of an abattoir in Bulgaria told its workers that there was no money for their wages – but that they would be paid in dead chickens. The company, in south-eastern Bulgaria, had tax arrears of about £740,000, but lots of lifeless poultry.

gambling debt in kind

A German man called the police after having to settle a gambling debt with his false teeth. The man, a resident of the city of Dortmund, told police that he was scared that he would have to live off liquid food until he had enough to buy new teeth. The police persuaded the other man involved to hand back the teeth when the first man promised to pay back the debt, worth about £100.

A Cambodian man bought three litres of petrol for his motorbike, then found he had left his wallet at home. He was on a trip with his nine-year-old nephew to try and find the boy's father. The man convinced the old lady who was selling petrol from her roadside stall to accept the boy in lieu of payment while he went to find the cash, the equivalent of about £1.00. Two years passed by, and the old lady finally realised that the man wasn't coming back, so she decided to raise the boy as her own grandson. Bargain – he gets three litres of petrol free, and she gets another mouth to feed.

Some sales people will try anything. The problem is when creative salesmanship gets sordid, as in the case of the 42-year-old tyre salesman for Tires Plus in the US state of Georgia, who was charged with offering a female customer four tyres in return for sex.

DRESS CODES

The manager of a Norwegian bank had a problem with the dress code for men, and decided that the traditional tie was 'alienating' to customers. So Mette Norbye Olsen, of the Postbanken in Tromsø, banned her male staff members from wearing them. 'Male staff will no longer be allowed to wear ties. They are a symbol of leadership and solemnity,' she said, not worrying about alienating any of her male staff who actually like wearing them.

 On the other hand ... or foot ... white socks were declared officially 'indecent' by the Dutch Finance Ministry. And to think white socks used to be a sign of purity. An internal publication proclaimed that white sports socks 'transgress the limits of decent dress behaviour' for ministry employees.

DREAM CAREERS

That's 'dream careers' as in 'in their dreams'.

Captain Kelsey McMillan arrived for duty at the RAF Valley base in Anglesey, North Wales, and her smart uniform and ID card won her crisp salutes from the security guards. McMillan told them she was a medical officer reporting for a retraining course; she went on to participate in training missions on Sea King helicopters, and worked in the hospital block. Popular in the officers' mess, with a reputation for generosity in the bar, McMillan turned out in reality to be an impostor with an obsession for uniforms, whose plausibility allowed her five whole blissful months at the base before she was discovered. McMillan had been no more than a private in the Territorials before her leap into the big time.

Medical

MEDICAL FISHINESS

Belgian Leo van Aert, 57, from Antwerp, was at home celebrating his birthday, but happiness gave way to despair as Leo's wife suddenly noticed that his beloved koi carp was acting strangely. Then it stopped moving altogether. Mr van Aert, a former ambulance driver,

Last June, as happens every year in the Indian city of Hyderabad, thousands of asthma sufferers congregate outside the home of the Goud family in the hope that they will be cured by swallowing live sardines covered with a secret herb blend. The exact date changes each year, since it is chosen by astrologers, and the treatment is free. The Goud family say that they learned the special herb recipe from a Hindu saint over 150 years ago. The yellow herbal paste is smeared inside the mouth of a live sardine – not inside the mouth of the asthma sufferer – and the sardine is swallowed by the patient with the help and 'special expertise' of a member of the Goud family.

ECCENTRIC

leaped into action. He took his pet fish from its tank, and, believing it to have suffered a heart attack, gave it heart massage. At first this seemed to help, but then once again the poor carp fell motionless. This time Mr van Aert gave the koi mouth-to-mouth resuscitation. The kiss of life lived up to its name, and the carp made a complete recovery.

BABIES

The birth of a child may often be seen as a miracle, but in this case the birth of baby Nhlahla in South Africa truly was a miracle. Nhlahla developed in her mother's liver instead of her womb. In around 1 in 100,000 pregnancies the fertilised egg implants some-where in the abdomen of the mother, but for a baby to develop in the liver and still survive is incredibly rare with only three other such cases on record. The birth was assisted by liver specialist Jack Krige who

In Beijing, a baby was born with a 100 per cent leg surplus. She had a third leg growing in her back, which was the leg of her undeveloped twin. Surgeons successfully removed the redundant limb.

reported that mother and baby were both doing well. Nhlahla weighed 2.8 kg (6 lb).

ASSORTED MARVELS

A 13-year-old boy was taken to hospital in West Bengal complaining that it hurt to pee. No wonder: astounded doctors discovered live winged beetles in his urine. The beetles were over half a centimetre long – it must *really* have hurt to pee them out – and appeared to come from eggs that had somehow been laid by a beetle inside the boy's body. Doctors were trying to work out how the beetle got in.

Wang Lixiang, a teacher in Beijing, was out in a field doing some planting, when he was struck by lightning. Unconscious, and with his clothes in tatters, he was taken to hospital where he lay in a coma for four days. When he came back to consciousness, he had been transformed into a memory man. The lightning strike had revved up his brain power so much that he was able to memorise huge strings of characters in just two or three scans. Wang didn't start a career on stage, though, choosing to remain a teacher.

In southern Turkey, a 46-year-old man finally gave in to reason and had an operation to remove a lump caused by a hernia. It wasn't a little lump – when doctors heaved it out of his body it weighed in at a massive 7 kg (15 lb). Mursel Demir had lived with the slowly growing lump for 20 years, reluctant to have surgery in case he died under the knife and left his children as orphans. But when his neighbours made fun of him because he looked as though he were pregnant – and his kids were grown up – he took the plunge.

An Indian man baffled doctors when it emerged that he had spent the last 68 years of life without eating or drinking (or going to the toilet, which I'm sure was your immediate question). Prahlad Jani, 76, was put under medical surveillance at a hospital in Ahmedabad for ten days and a team of doctors was unable to disprove his claim that he never eats or drinks. There was some evidence that urine formed in his bladder but was reabsorbed through the bladder wall. Jani claims that he 'gets the elixir of life' through a hole in his palate between his mouth and nose. One of the hospital doctors has urged Jani to be tested by NASA, in case his skills could come in handy for astronauts.

From non-eater to non-sleeper: doctors in Romania were also baffled when they dealt with the case of a woman who said that she had not slept for eight years. Maria Stelica, 54, developed insomnia after the death of her mother eight years ago, fearing that she would dream about her mother. Gradually she came to be able to do without sleep altogether, and after doctors ran a series of clinical tests, they said that her case appeared to be genuine, and that they could offer no explanation for eight sleepless years.

A 23-year-old woman from Sichuan province in China was dumped by her boyfriend when he discovered she had no anus. Song Yai's parents had not told her that she was different from other girls and for her whole life she had happily defecated through her vagina. Surgeons swiftly rectified the situation, creating an anus for her and Song is now whole. We don't know whether her boyfriend has taken her back.

medical maggots

A new, state-of-the-art hospital in Scotland introduced a somewhat medieval form of treatment for diabetic patients – maggots. The New Edinburgh Royal Infirmary started buying in maggots from a Welsh company and using them to eat dead flesh on dirty, infected lesions, leaving a clean wound that begins to heal. Matthew Young, a diabetes consultant at the hospital, stated that maggots provide a gentler and quicker way of cleaning a wound.

VANITY AND THE KNIFE

Last year we reported on a new South Korean trend for tongue surgery to help them speak English better. This year the trend in that country appears to be an altogether different form of gratuitous operation: pubic hair enhancement surgery. Yes, while women all over the world trim, clip and wax their pubic hair to make it look less like a garden hedge, South Korean women are prepared to pay around £1,500 to have hair transplanted from their heads to their muffs. Bushiness is regarded as a sign of fertility, so luxuriant growth means more chance of trapping a husband.

It pays to be consistent with your cosmetic surgery – and it certainly pays the cosmetic surgeons. Once you've had your jawline tightened, and your nose job, and your wrinkles stretched out, you still might sound old – even though you look young and fresh, and not at all like you've had lots of work done. So you have plastic surgery on your voice. Yes, this is the new trend capturing the imagination of those who will pay what it costs to stop appearing to age. Two procedures have been developed to stop your tremulous voice giving away your true age. One is implants that bring the vocal cords closer together; the other is an injection of collagen that makes the cords plumper. Both will make you sound years younger as you ask the sales girl to bring you more Prada outfits.

A 30-year-old Chinese man in the central Hubei province emerged victorious in a Mr Ugly competition (in case you can't guess, that's like a beauty contest, but in reverse). The man was so ugly, apparently, that it caused him to lose his job, and, at the age of 30, he had 'never had a romantic experience'. His prize as the city of Wuhan's Mr Ugly was three months of plastic surgery to make him look like one of China's most popular singers, Lu Yi.

An American by the name of Michael J. Tito won an online vote on a TV makeover show and was treated to the surgery necessary to transform him into the star he most admired: Jennifer Lopez. Tito had jaw and brow sculpting, bottom implants (of course!) and cheek implants, not to mention hormone treatment and breast enlargement. Tito, who planned to change his name to Jessica (why not go the whole hog and choose Jennifer, we want to know?), said he was pleased with the results – but no one had actually thought he was J-Lo.

BOTCHED OPS

Getting the dose of anaesthetic right in major operations is tricky. If the patient wakes up early, it's not pretty. At a hospital in Oakland, Pennsylvania, a 35-year-old man having a kidney transplanted from his mother woke up from his anaesthesia and suddenly sat bolt upright. The just-sewn-in kidney was forced up with such power that it ripped an artery and protruded from his abdomen. The kidney could no longer be used and was removed the next day.

medical creativity

A surgeon in the town of Andahuaylas, Peru, was making the best of his hospital's lack of funds to buy proper surgical instruments by using a variety of builders' tools to operate on patients. Doctor Cesar Venero carried out one of his operations, for example, using a drill and a pair of pliers. A hospital spokesman reassured questioners that the equipment was sterilised, and praised the doctor's approach as being cheap and creative.

Science & Technology

INVENTIONS

Scientists in Japan spent about £600,000 on building a toy for fish enthusiasts: a robotic koi carp. Real koi are often a target for thieves, and rare specimens can fetch up to £50,000. The Robocarp is the size of a fully grown fish, weighing 20 kg (40 lb) and measuring 3 ft in length. It lives in a special tank that transmits signals to sensors in the fish to make it swim about in a completely realistic way.

Skivers and adulterers rejoice – a Romanian firm has created an 'audible alibi' for mobile phones, so callers can pretend they are somewhere they are not. The background sounds on offer include 'at the park', 'at the dentist', 'on the street' and even 'circus parade', though let's face it, that last one's going to need a bit of explaining to the missus. Simedia, a Romania-based phone software company, has innovated an 'audible alibi', which can be used to deceive callers at the other end. The software, SounderCover, can reportedly mimic a thunderstorm, the dentist's drill or even a circus during a call to avoid one of those pretentiously boring conversations. Different backgrounds can also be assigned to different phone numbers so that they automatically kick in when a certain person calls. The trick involves blending the outgoing voice audio with another looped audio track.

American Kevin Rymer invented the CatSeat last year. It's a device that will train cats to use the toilet in a house. It's similar to a toilet seat, with a box attached which is textured to feel like cat litter. The kittyshitkit, as I like to call it, starts in place of the cat's own litter tray, then eventually can be mounted on the toilet in the house. A push of a button makes the toilet usable by humans. So if you'd like to share the toilet with your cat, and save a fortune on cat litter, get a CatSeat. My cat uses the back garden, by the way.

CLOTHING INNOVATIONS

After news of last year's moisturising bras comes news of an emergency bra. And panic pants. A group of scientists in Germany came up with underwear embedded with tiny sensors that can monitor heart rhythms and, in the case of heart problems, send signals to a control unit which passes on the call to the emergency services, giving details of the wearer's location.

Swiss-based underwear maker Triumph International developed an anti-smoking bra. Triumph claims the bra will help women quit smoking thanks to perfumed capsules which give cigarettes an unpleasant taste and soothe withdrawal symptoms. The capsules contain lavender scent, which has sedative properties, as well as normally sweet-smelling jasmine that alters the taste of cigarettes, and the bra is also treated with liquid titanium to break down cigarette smoke.

Tights that help you lose weight made a brief appearance in European shops – brief because they sold out so quickly. In some stores the Slim Fit tights were selling faster than shops could put them on the shelves, entire stocks selling out within a week. The tights, created by Palmers at the University of Vienna, look like ordinary tights but have a crucial difference – they are impregnated with specially created microscopic capsules of gelatine which contain caffeine. The heat from the human body and contact with the skin allows the caffeine to be slowly released as the gelatine breaks down. Caffeine speeds up the metabolism and increases the breakdown of fat. Actually, exercise does this too. So why not just put on an old pair of tights, ladies, and walk to your nearest coffee bar?

Not so much a clothing innovation as a trend reflecting market demand: US lingerie retailer Torrid last year upsized its sexy underwear range to feed the demand for overfed young women who think that squeezing into a thong makes them look sexy (and not even more enormous). Torrid brought out bikinis, thongs and camisoles that went up to an elephantine size 26 – and profits grew fatter.

the bleedin' obvious

Taking the boundaries of human knowledge that little bit further ... scientists at the University of Malawi carried out an experiment that proved this amazing fact: chocolate tastes better when you are hungry. Another research grant well spent.

Art

Where do you draw the line in modern art between serious and weird? It's very hard. We go by gut instinct.

A Dutch artist, Joanneke Meester, from Amsterdam expressed her concern at the rising levels of violence in society by creating a tiny gun – out of her own skin. Meester had a 20-centimetre square of skin sliced away from her stomach, and used it to cover a small gun made out of plastic. Commenting on her work, Meester said that she had no choice but to use her own skin.

Toronto artist Jason Kronewald received a bit of attention in the news last year thanks to his portraits of celebrities. These are no ordinary portraits: Kronewald sculpts them from hundreds of pieces of used chewing gum. He doesn't chew the gum himself – he gets friends to do the jaw work to produce the raw material that contributed to his 'Gum Blondes' series, including portraits of Pamela Anderson and Britney Spears.

The Sweet Productions theatre company put on a play at the Edinburgh Fringe Festival that

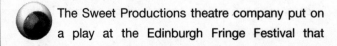

really was way beyond the fringe. *Sweet FA* goes like this: audience comes in, sits down, and the house lights go down. Sixty minutes pass. Nothing happens. Repeat, nothing happens. No actors come on stage. Then the house lights come up again and the audience, if there is anyone left, leaves. At least you wouldn't forget the plot.

At the time of going to print the play had not yet been staged, so we can't say whether the weird casting was successful: a theatre group auditioned for someone who would be dead by the time the production was staged, so that they could play the part of a corpse to 'lie in state' for the whole performance. The play, called *Dead: You Will Be*, was conceived by an experimental theatre group in East London, and the casting call was sent round to local hospices in the hope of finding a terminally ill patient who would rise to the challenge.

A Welsh poet by the name of Karl Beer was given a grant to help fund his latest artistic project – to write about binge drinking. Mr Beer – apparently his real name – was awarded £2,500 of Lottery money, but in his home town of Port Talbot, where resources are thin on the ground, an artist being given all that money in order to go out and get blind drunk on a regular basis was not popular.

UK sculptor Alistair Mackie gets some of his materials for free by collecting owl pellets. Owls eat their prey whole then regurgitate pellets containing the indigestible stuff, and it is precisely this that Mackie is after, in the form of mouse skulls. He prises the skulls out of the tightly packed pellets, cleans them, bleaches them and then superglues them together into shapes such as a hollow sphere. His sculptures sell for up to £3,000.

LIFE IMITATING ART

There's a horror film – *Christine* – about a car with a mind of its own (*Herbie* is also a film about a car with a mind of its own, but it's hardly a horror film – horrific, maybe), and in the US state of Colorado 20-year-old Angel Eck found herself at the mercy of her speeding Pontiac on Interstate 70. The car locked itself into overdrive and accelerated to 100 mph. She couldn't disengage the ignition, since that was stuck too, and Angel was saved by two canny cops who overtook the wilful Pontiac and gradually slowed down in front of it. A few days later, in a mechanic's workshop the car was sitting with its engine idling. Obviously, it waited until a mechanic was in front of it, then jumped the gears, jerked forward and pinned him to the wall. He was rescued by a colleague. That Pontiac must be destroyed now, with a crucifix and a silver bullet, before it strikes again.

Travel Tales

What would you expect to visit when travelling to the mystical East? Spectacular temples and pagodas? Exotic markets? A sewage works? Singapore's latest tourist attraction is a sewage conversion plant. The plant's visitor centre became so popular that the city government decided to offer it on the list of Singapore sights to see, putting it alongside the famous Raffles Hotel and the Singapore Zoo. In ten months, the plant, which purifies sewage water into drinking water, had 100,000 visitors; and government officials have had themselves photographed drinking the converted water as proof that it is not only harmless, but that it tastes good too.

Passengers on London's creaking Underground train system are no strangers to delays. But one delay had a cause that no one could ever have imagined – a vasectomy. A trainee driver, listening to one of his colleagues talking frankly about his vasectomy, fainted in the cab of a train leaving Aldgate Station, sustaining

After unsuccessfully trying to wake the occupant of an illegally parked car, a traffic warden in Melbourne, Australia, issued a $100 parking ticket and tiptoed away, desperately hoping that the man was not going to cut up rough. No chance of that – Robbie LaRocca, inside the car, was not sleeping but dead, having taken an overdose, and had been slumped in the driver's seat for several hours. The warden had thought he was drunk and didn't want the parking ticket to set off a nasty confrontation.

head and chest injuries which meant the train had to be stopped and the poor, squeamish young chap had to be taken to hospital. Thousands of passengers were delayed as the Hammersmith and City and Circle lines were brought to a standstill due, London Underground said at the time, to a 'defective train'.

Commuters don't like their journey home to be disrupted, but for one American man the daily homeward train ride became a nightmare. Edwin Gallard had gone to the toilet on a train travelling out of New York City to the Connecticut suburbs, and was making a call on his mobile phone. He dropped his mobile, and it landed in the toilet bowl, disappearing from view round the bend. So he shoved first his hand, then his arm after it, with the simple result that he became firmly and immovably stuck there. Railway staff were unable to help him, so the train was stopped and police officers and firefighters joined in the fun, eventually having to resort to cutting equipment to slice open the toilet and free him. The track had to be closed, and thousands of commuters were heavily delayed during the evening rush hour. And the mobile phone had slithered away into a chemical tank, where there was no retrieving it anyway.

Road rage and high blood pressure go alongside the possibility of accidents as inescapable parts of travelling by car, so the RAC came up with a list of music NOT to listen to while driving. And top of the list was Richard Wagner's 'Ride of the Valkyries', surprisingly, being deemed to be likely to cause accidents, while the more overtly aggressive 'Firestarter' by The Prodigy was also included in the top five. You have been warned.

A Swedish bus driver neatly skipped round petty regulations that prevented him from cooling off as temperatures in the driving seat rose in summer sunshine. Mats Lundgren, of the town of Umea, requested permission to wear shorts in one of Sweden's hottest summers, but the transport company's dress code forbade it. Lundgren slipped on a sober and discreet navy-blue skirt, and drove his bus with his legs out in the open as he desired. And a careful reading of the rulebook showed that since skirts were one of the company's accepted types of dress, and there was no mention of whether men were or were not allowed to wear them, he got his way. And to his credit, the MD of the transport authority said that unusual as it was to see a man in a skirt driving a bus, he would do nothing about it.

An earlier *Another Weird Year* story had a man hijacking a London bus and telling the driver to take him to the place that the bus happened to be going to anyway. This year a court case has revealed that a while ago, 62-year-old Auburn Mason, on a British Airways flight from Trinidad, held a pair of scissors to the neck of a flight attendant, told all and sundry that he was hijacking the plane, and demanded to be flown to London's Gatwick airport. In fact, the plane was only 15 minutes from landing at its scheduled destination – London Gatwick.

WELSH RAREBIT

A road accident occurred in Wales that had all the ingredients of a cheesy gag. A lorry carrying ten tons of cheese had a fire on board, and the cheese was turned into a giant fondue. Firefighters fought the flames for over an hour as the load of melted cheese flowed like high-cholesterol lava onto the A44 near Aberystwyth; police closed the road and told motorists to divert to Caerphilly.

Pranks

In sober-sided Switzerland a practical joker gained access to a public announcement system and successfully fooled over 50 commuters on the Bern to Neuenberg train. A special announcement came just as the train pulled into the tiny station of Kerzers, telling commuters that the journey to Neuenberg had to be continued by bus. More than 50 commuters left the train, then watched in dismay as it left them on the platform. Obviously, there was no bus.

Now I'm assuming that this story was a prank of an impressively depraved nature, but we don't know for sure. Staff at a Berlin aquarium discovered that their petting pool, a special pool where children can touch friendly sea creatures, had a new and far from benign addition – a piranha fish. The piranha had already started taking bites out of other fish in the pool, and was so speedy that the whole pool had to be vacated and emptied before staff could trap it and take it safely away to another aquarium. Its appearance in the pool was a complete mystery.

ODD

Shanna Hill and Jerry Routon were friends and roommates, in the Colorado town of Louisville. One evening Jerry took out the rubbish while Shanna got her car ready to drive them to a restaurant. When she drove into the car park in front of their block of flats, she couldn't see him, and knowing that he was always playing pranks and had probably run off and hidden, she drove swiftly past their meeting point, feeling the familiar thump of a speed bump under her car as she did so. Except speed bumps don't scream in agony when you drive over them. It wasn't a speed bump – it was Jerry. Lying down in the car park hadn't been such a good trick to play after all. Fortunately, Jerry survived, though he's probably more careful about where he plays pranks these days.

BACKFIRING PRANKS

In the city of Spokane, in the US state of Washington, two young men drove to a fast-food restaurant in the early hours of a freezing January morning, stripped off, leapt out of the car, which they left idling, and cavorted naked around the restaurant. One of the customers swiftly nipped out, got into their car and drove off. The car turned up five days later, with no clothes to be seen.

A man in the US state of New York played a macabre April Fool on his ex-wife with such devastating effect that he faced criminal charges. Randy Wood of Oswego County phoned his ex-wife to say he had something to show her. When she went to his house she found him hanging by the neck from a tree in his front garden. He had secured himself with a hidden harness, but his ex-wife was fooled to the extent that she called 911 and alerted the emergency services.

Superstitious Nonsense

THE THINGS PEOPLE BELIEVE ...

A Chinese man in south-western Sichuan province was told by a fortune-teller – a pretty weird fortune-teller, by the sound of it – that the only way for him to cure his ailing wife was to feed her human body parts. That was back in 1988, and after 16 years of grave-robbing, the 51-year-old was finally apprehended. He was arrested for having stolen 30 corpses from local cemeteries, making soup from the flesh and grinding the bones to make a powder to brush onto her fore-head, as the fortune-teller also told him to do. It is not known what his wife's illness was, but she certainly didn't get better straight away, or he wouldn't have gone on taking bodies.

In New York City, a 50-year-old woman was admitted to hospital with stomach pains. On examination, it turned out that she had inserted pieces of chicken into her womb then safety-pinned her vagina shut, in the hope that the chicken would grow to be a baby.

A Romanian man, Mircea Teodarescu, visited a fortune-teller, and received a piece of news that rocked him back: either he, said the fortune-teller, or his son, would die before the week as out. So Teodarescu did the decent thing – he slit his own throat, reasoning that thus his son would not be the one to die.

In Nigeria, a doctor faced, and failed, the acid test. Ashi Terfa had prepared an anti-bullet charm for a patient, then tied it round his own neck. The patient, Umaa Akor, then fired a gun at his head to test the charm's effectiveness. To everyone's amazement, Terfa was shot dead. Akor was charged with culpable homicide and released on bail; police said the motive to kill could not be established as the doctor had asked him to shoot him to test the charm.

There are unlucky numbers and lucky numbers. And an unidentified bidder on an online auction in China apparently paid nearly £1 million for a mobile phone number. The number, 135 8585 8585 is pronounced the same as 'let me be rich, be rich, be rich'. With a million spare for a mobile phone number, I think the buyer was missing the point a little.

The shrine of a Muslim saint in north-western Pakistan was where thousands of toothache sufferers made their way last year, safe in the knowledge that simply by visiting the shrine of Amir Ghazi Baba and then hammering a nail into a plank their pain would cease. The shrine became so famous that people in the area stopped going to see their dentists, and went to the shrine instead.

RELIGIOUS NONSENSE

Tickets at a cinema in the US state of Georgia caused an unholy row when some filmgoers noticed a certain devilish number on them. The film was *The Passion of Christ*, starring Mel Gibson, and the number, which appeared at the beginning of a string of numbers on each and every ticket, was 666. The film depicts the last hours of Christ's life, including the crucifixion, and some people who bought tickets complained that the number of the devil, 666, appeared on their tickets, even though the number sequence was computer-generated.

George Bothwell, a farmer in Ontario, took the state government to court for insisting that he have a photo taken to be put on his new driving licence. Bothwell believes that the Book of Revelation (which is where the 666 idea comes from) cites such images – also fingerprints – as the work of the devil. Anyone who has their imaged stored by an outside agency, he says, will 'bear the mark of the beast' and suffer the wrath of God. So no driving licence for him, then.

In the county of Lincolnshire God was asked to lend a hand with council work when the Bishop of Lincoln blessed the council's gritting lorries in an attempt to cut road deaths in icy weather. The Right Rev. Dr John Saxbee led prayers at a gritting depot in the city of Lincoln, while simultaneous services were held at eight other depots around the county. Dr Saxbee asked God to be with all drivers at that treacherous time of the year, when icy roads lead to hundreds of road accidents. The idea was that as the salt was spread by the gritters, the road safety blessing would be extended onto the county's road network. Police Chief Inspector Paul Elliott, who came up with the idea, asked churches across the county to hold a prayer session, coinciding with a full gritting operation, to strengthen the blessing's power.

A clothes shop in the US state of Pennsylvania caused outrage when it started selling a new line of novelty toys. Magnetic Jesus Dress Up! is an image of Jesus – on the cross, wearing Y-fronts – that can be dressed up in a variety of outfits, such as a tutu, a devil suit or a hula skirt. Harmless fun, or maybe blasphemy – it all depends. Anyway, predictably, a group of Catholic protesters braved freezing winds outside the shopping mall where the 'blasphemous' toy was on sale, to protest and to try to dissuade shoppers from going into Urban Outfitters, the nasty store in question.

LIFE'S LITTLE IRONIES

Mañana, always mañana. The President of Ecuador, Lucio Gutierrez, fronted a campaign to deal with his nation's famous lack of interest in punctuality. He was to be interviewed on Teleamazonas TV, but he turned up late.

Gary Collins of Wagga Wagga, Australia, appeared on local television to complain about the dangers of a stretch of road in Big Springs, nearby. It was only a matter of time, he said, before there was fatal accident. How right he was – the very next day, Collins, riding his four-wheel motorcycle, was killed instantly when he crashed into a school bus on that very stretch of road.

The Japanese government launched an ad campaign to urge the public to pay their pension contributions, something which is obligatory in Japan. Thirty thousand posters were printed, featuring a well-known actress, Makiko Esumi, and a TV ad starring her was also aired. Then, of course, it turned out that Esumi had not paid any pension contributions for two years, and owed about £1,700.

QUIRKY

Firefighters in the town of Melbourne, Florida, had to respond to a string of emergency calls, and returned to their fire station to find it ablaze. One of the firefighters had left a pan with oil in it heating on the stove. The station was gutted, and probably the firefighters were too.

In Marion prison, in the US state of Ohio, Willie Chapman, inside on a manslaughter charge, got permission to delay his scheduled parole by one day so he could attend a prison meeting of the religious/personal responsibility organisation Promise Keepers. Now the irony was that by being extra good, he made the newspapers. And the parents of Chapman's manslaughter victim read about him coming out on parole. And they immediately complained to the Ohio Parole Board. And the Ohio Parole Board reconsidered Chapman's parole and delayed it 991 days, until 1 May 2006.

A minister in the Danish Parliament's road safety commission was forced to resign when he was caught speeding. Jakob Buksti was clocked at over 100 mph in a 70 mph speed limit area. As Minister for Transport, Buksti had urged motorists not to exceed speed limits, and had also criticised the centre-right government for increasing the speed limit on a large proportion of Denmark's roads from 110 kph to 130 kph.

An apple a day keeps the doctor ... coming back to you, in the case of Linda Mitchell from Sheffield. The 56-year-old discovered that 25 years of eating apples and 25 years of migraines and stomach problems were no coincidence. It was the apples that made her ill.

A small comedy club in south London was obliged to shut down – not because it wasn't funny enough, but because, ironically, it was too funny. The Manor Arms in Clapham was rocked by gales of laughter every week when the Comedy Pit club was staged, to the disgust of local residents who complained about the noise. Council officers checked the noise levels and indeed the laughter was too loud.

You couldn't make it up ... A man in eastern Russia parked his brand-new £70,000 jeep outside a church and went inside to get blessed for a safe drive home. And you've guessed it – when he came out his shiny new car had been nicked, along with his video camera and over £2,000 in cash. Police found the man in such a state of shock he had to be taken to hospital.

Jaap van Zyl, 57, swam out to sea off the coast of Hermanus, South Africa, to scatter the ashes of his deceased father. He was with his son, Jaco, but Jaco was not near enough to his father to help him when Jaap was overcome by cramp and was sucked beneath the waves to his death – with his father's ashes still in his hand. We suggest Jaco doesn't swim out to scatter his father's ashes ...

In the Alaskan city of Homer, Robert Keys, a local businessman, stood up in the city council chambers to protest against a ban on smoking in the city. An ex-smoker, he told the crowded meeting that he sat with a group of smokers for coffee and a chat every single morning, and that it had absolutely no effect on his heart or his health, and that a non-smoking policy should be optional. Keys then sat

and a very big irony

In Australia, a convicted murderer, Paul Charles Denyer, told police when he was arrested that he had picked three women to kill because he 'just hates women'. Next thing you know Denyer, inside Barwon Prison, applied for hormone treatment and surgery to become a woman.

down. Not five minutes later, he collapsed and died of a heart attack.

A woman in the US state of Massachusetts had a fatal accident while driving and speaking on her mobile at the same time. The irony was that when she lost control of her car she crashed into Cingular Wireless, a mobile phone shop.

WHAT'S IN A NAME?

He put down $40 in Las Vegas at the World Series of Poker, and walked away with the title and a pot of $2.5 million. His name? Chris Moneymaker. The 27-year-old from Tennessee qualified for the competition on the Internet and bluffed his way to a fortune.

A New Zealand outdoor clothing company was obliged to change its brand name for the Australian market. Market research showed that Aussie men were more than reluctant – scared, even – to wear clothes that bore the name 'Fairydown', even though it was the brand of choice for Sir Edmund Hillary, the great mountaineer. To save Australian men the embarrassment of having the Fairydown label – and to sell the stuff – Fairydown branded its Aussie gear as 'Zone'. Nice and macho.

There is an Italian battery company called Powergen. And 'Italy' in Italian is 'Italia'. And all big companies have websites. So the web address for this company, which has caused a fair amount of amusement in English-speaking circles this last year, is www.powergenitalia.com.

An American, Thomas Frank White, living in Thailand, was accused of having had sex with underage children; to fight extradition, he hired a Thai lawyer whose name was Kittyporn Arunrat.

This cute little catalogue will sound like it comes from a Disney film, but it was noted at the Greenhill Primary School in Sheffield. The crossing supervisor,

Product names are a potential can of worms in these days of global marketing. The famous old gaffes include KFC's slogan 'Finger Lickin' Good' going into China as 'Eat your fingers off', and Vauxhall's Nova car meaning 'doesn't go' in Spanish. This year, UK food company Sharwoods joined in with its new 'Bundh' range of Indian sauces unaware that in Punjabi, 'bundh' means 'arse'.

Jon Blake Cusack, an engineering geek (his own words) from Michigan, talked his wife, Jamie, into naming their son Jon Blake Cusack 2.0. Version 2.0 was born bearing features from version 1.0, with additional features integrated from mother Jamie. She finally gave in to her husband's request to name their baby version 2.0 just one week before the birth, reasoning that since she had had control over the decoration of the baby's room, she should let her husband have his way.

BIZARRE

who sees the kids safely across the street every morning, is Alan Rhodes. Class then starts, to the sound of a bell, rung by teacher Linda Bell. Teachers of reading and writing are Jane Reid and Graham Wright, while music is taught by Heather Tune, helped by Ian Sharp (presumably only on the higher notes). IT classes are led by Sue Smart and Emma Wise, while the caretaker, whose job it is to vacuum the floors, is a Mr Dyson.

Researchers at the British National Archive came across a weirdly prophetic name. Way back in 1379, a Mr and Mrs Coke named their daughter Dionisia (in modern times 'Denise'), which in those days was typically shortened to Diot. Enter the first ever Diot Coke.

really dangerous name

When a car slid into the Huallaga River in Peru's Amazon region four people were drowned. One of the dead was a four-year-old boy by the name of Adolpho Hitler. His father, Manuel Garcia, had named his first son Adolpho Hitler, 'in honour of a historical figure', but he had drowned in the same river 11 years earlier. Garcia gave his second son the same name, with, amazingly, the same unhappy result.

REALLY STUPID NAMES

A few names that were given to unsuspecting babies during the last year. Babies just don't know what they're being saddled with. Far be it for me to be judgemental – but these names, revealed in a discussion group, are mental. Cam'ron. Yes, spelled like that. Twins called Kiarne Rhukaya and Paris Jewel. A girl called Meander. Nevaeh – which is stupid enough without you knowing that it's 'heaven' spelled backwards. Gennavieve Luaraleigh, whose mother said, not surprisingly, that, 'I still have not come across any babies with that name yet.' Pookie Bair and Poopsie Dier were another pair of twins who will be swept through life on a gale of contemptuous laughter.

And just a snippet pulled from a survey of names given to babies in the US last year with a rather sordid feel to them: three were named Latrine, and one was named Chlamydia. While brand names were passed on to a few boys who were called Courvoisier, and another little crop named Del Monte.

HIDDEN-AWAY PEOPLE

A Romanian man hid away in the basement of his house for an amazing eleven years in an attempt to avoid a prison sentence for trying to kill one of his neighbours. The 31-year-old claimed he was innocent, but after a tip-off to the police he was arrested again this year. The original prison sentence, given eleven years ago, was for just eight years. Oh dear.

Over two whole decades ago, an Iraqi man was put under an execution order by Saddam Hussein for supporting a Shia cleric (in a country where Sunni Islam is the predominant branch). Jawad Amir immediately went into hiding, in a tiny space between two walls in his parents' home. For 21 long years he lived in this space with just a few possessions, including a radio on which he eventually heard about the overthrow of Saddam, after which he felt it was safe to come out.

MAD MAILING

Charles D. McKinley was living in New York City, but was homesick for his home town of Dallas, Texas. To save money on the trip, McKinley, 25, loaded himself into a crate at the warehouse where he worked, had a form filled out to say the crate contained a computer and clothing, and posted himself as airline cargo to his parents' house. At the end of the 15-hour journey, McKinley broke out of the crate, to the amazement of his parents and the deliveryman. He had taken no food or water for his journey, just a mobile phone that didn't work. Luckily for McKinley, his crate was not carried in an unpressurised hold, where he could have frozen to death. And for the $550 that the freight cost his employers, he could have flown first class. McKinley was arrested shortly after his shock homecoming – he had cheque fraud and traffic offences hanging over him – and federal officials were also contemplating criminal charges for his stowaway ride.

A Colombian man did the Trojan horse trick in an attempt to burgle a huge house in the gangster-ridden, cocaine-baron city of Medellin. He hid inside a large box and posted himself to the house. The owners not surprisingly got suspicious, and called up the bomb squad, who found a man armed with a gun and a knife, but weak and gasping for air.

TATTOO TALES

In the South Korean capital of Seoul 170 men were arrested on charges of getting tattooed. The problem? They were using the tattoos to get out of doing military service. It isn't technically illegal to have a tattoo, but South Koreans see them as symbols of disgrace, usually associated with gangsters. The country's conscription law says men with large tattoos are unfit for military service because they cause 'abomination among fellow

A tattoo artist in Idaho has started winning over an entirely new and rather unconventional – even for a tattoo artist – customer base: horses. Teri Reid, who calls herself a specialist in permanent cosmetics, is visited by horse owners not because they want cool, tattooed horses, but because Teri can provide a particular service. So-called 'paint' horses have very light colouring, and there is no natural pigmentation around the eyes. This can lead to long-term problems from sunlight exposure, like cataracts and sunburn, so Teri is called upon to tattoo a black line around the horse's eyes – just like permanent eyeliner – to deflect the sun's glare.

soldiers'. So the actual charges were 'wilfully tampering with their bodies to avoid military duty'.

A Leeds man went into hospital for heart surgery, which involved the removal of a part of a vein in his leg. His bold statement tattoo, 'I love women' (maybe stating the obvious, maybe a little too defensive?) was, sadly, just over the spot the surgeon had to cut. After the incision was sewn up, part of the tattoo disappeared, so that when he came out of hospital his macho statement now read 'I love men.'

TWINS

Madelaine Jones married Roy Littlejohns in 1980, and her identical twin sister Michele was of course the first person she invited to the wedding. Roy and Madelaine enjoyed eight years of relatively uneventful life in Northampton until Madelaine went into hospital after a series of epileptic fits. Twin sister Michelle became Roy's housekeeper while Madelaine was in hospital, and then eight years later Roy and Madelaine split up. Shortly afterwards Roy told Madelaine that Michelle was moving in with him, and the twins had a furious row when Madelaine discovered that Roy and Michelle had journeyed to Las Vegas to get married. Roy had married both twins, 23 years apart. His verdict? 'My relationship with Michelle is more romantic.' The sisters have since made up.

robin hood stuff

A Romanian robber was caught in the act – not of robbing but of handing out the booty to homeless people. The 30-year-old, from Iasi, was arrested in a hostel where he was found giving clothes, jewellery and money to poor people, having robbed a store a week earlier of goods worth about £1,000.

In the US state of Nebraska eight-year-old twins Cassidy and Marissa Wiese did that weird twin thing of sustaining the same injury on the same day in different parts of the neighbourhood, doing the same thing. Cassidy broke her left arm rollerskating at a friend's birthday party, and a few hours later Marissa was practising her rollerskating skills and also broke her left arm. Spooky. The girls were kitted out afterwards in matching blue plaster casts.

PARANOIA

The following chain of events may seem totally outrageous – it just shows how the minds of people in authority can be addled by paranoia. When a young American schoolboy started making 'violent' sketches, the paranoid alarm system was set clanging at full volume. In the rural backwater of Prosser, Washington state, a 15-year-old boy drew pictures for an art assignment that called for an end to the war in Iraq, urged people to vote for the Green Party and showed acts of violence committed by Arabs on President George W. Bush. So what happened? First the school principal did the patriotic (paranoid?) thing and called the police. The police, clearly with the interests of national security at heart, faxed the sketches to the Secret Service. Members of the Secret Service, probably dressed in black, then flew to Prosser to interview the boy. School principal Kevin Lusk said he was concerned that the student – who has no history of anti-social behaviour –

Not just superstitious but paranoid too: two American Legion posts and two other veterans' groups in the Californian town of Pleasanton sponsored a class on dowsing to see if domestic terrorists could be identified by pointing sticks at them; the idea being that the dowsing stick would wobble in the presence of an evil terrorist. As one of the leaders put it: 'You can't wait for the FBI and police to come up with solutions when you have the bad guys living among us.'

could pose a threat to Mr Bush. After the interviews by the Men in Black, the student was not suspended, but he was disciplined. God Bless America.

FALSE ALARMS

One evening in the Russian town of Yukhnov, a 16-year-old boy, out with his friends, received a frantic call on his mobile phone. It was from his father, warning him not to come home because there was a UFO outside their flat and if he did come home he would be abducted by aliens. The boy went and stood outside his apartment block and had a look. No spacecraft. He called his father and told him, but his father said he could still see it – and aliens were descending from it. So he bravely went into his family's flat, where he found that his mother had left a kettle of boiling water on the stove, which had put out the flame on the gas cooker, and the gas that was still coming out was giving them all hallucinations.

NAKEDNESS

We told you in the very first edition of *Another Weird Year* about an Indian boy who refused to wear clothes. Last year the story of a Cambodian boy, Sen Phana, emerged. He's 17 now and goes by the nickname of 'Para srat', which as you all know means in Khmer 'the man with no clothes', because he has refused to wear a stitch of clothing since he was about one year old. Because he has not been allowed in school naked, he is barely literate. This is a young man who has really decided to follow his own path in life, since he also refuses to have his hair cut, so he has 17 years' growth that has suffered the occasional trim. His mother said that when he has his hair cut short his character changes and he tries to kill chickens and ducks. Phana has never disclosed his reasons for staying unclothed, and has resisted persuasive gifts from neighbours and relatives and beatings from his father all aimed at getting him to put something on. Phana was reported to have said to his father: 'Even if you beat me till I am dead, I won't wear clothes.'

A man amazed onlookers (and fitness experts too, probably) by carrying out the double feat of running naked around the Chinese city of Changcun in sub-zero temperatures, for five hours. The nude multi-marathoner was eventually hauled in by police, but didn't appear to be exhausted. Maybe he'd just had a really long sauna.

Since, as we all know, early Christians were nudists, a Christian nudist resort opened in Florida. Founder Bill Martin points out key moments of Christian nudity, such as Jesus being nude when he

In the downtown area of the Florida town of Key West, a restaurant opened that was believed to be America's first 'clothing-optional' eatery not located in a nudist camp. Its name? Naked Lunch.

washed the apostles' feet and Peter being nude when he was in his fishing boat, which seem perfectly good reasons for living a nude Christian life.

In the Chinese city of Guangzhou, a woman made her husband pay for having a row with her by taking off every stitch of clothing and running out into the street. The woman's husband was then to be seen running after her, apologising profusely to everyone she passed and trying to get her to come back indoors. He was even more embarrassed when a massive traffic jam of spectators formed and eventually police were called to deal with things.

The American state of Minnesota gets very cold in winter, but that didn't stop a piece of naughty (in

Ever thought you needed a new angle on brushing up on your conversational French or German? According to Jesse Au King-wai, the way forward in language teaching is ... nude teachers. So if you live in Hong Kong you benefit from having a man who runs an adult TV channel who is prepared to make nudity educational as well as entertaining.

the criminal sense) nudity. On Christmas morning last year, a naked man was found stuck in the chimney of a bookshop in Minneapolis. A passer-by alerted police after hearing screams for help, and after breaking into the shop and destroying part of the chimney, police were able to rescue the 34-year-old man, who had climbed onto the shop's roof to burgle the store, stripped off his clothes so as to make his entry easier, and climbed down the chimney. The man's excuse was that he had dropped his keys down the chimney and was trying to retrieve them.

 The journey from Land's End to John O'Groats is one that has been attempted in a huge variety of ways. Stephen Gough walked it, which is nothing new, but he did so naked, which is definitely novel, especially since he was arrested for breach of the peace several times during his odyssey. Gough set out on the walk at the height of summer, as a celebration of the human body and to try and alter people's perceptions about nakedness. He did allow himself to wear walking boots and socks, and as temperatures dropped, a hat (on his head). Arriving at Scotland's northernmost tip in freezing January rain, Gough took a swift dip in the sea to mark the end of his six-month slog.

You'd think grown adults in a sophisticated liberal society would not find nudity exceptional. But then this story does come from Texas: a boat carrying 60 passengers across Lake Travis, near Austin, capsized when the passengers all ran over to one side of the boat at the same time in order to gawp at a load of naked sunbathers on a nudist beach. Two passengers were injured, but they did get the thrill of having some of the nudists swim out to help rescue them.

POO

There are always a few poo-based incidents each year to keep you happy.

Lightning struck a school in Angara, India, and the school principal found 15 students unconscious in the school hall. He called doctors, but before they could arrive and minister to the poor students, the students were taken out of the school by villagers and covered in cow dung, this being the local cure for being struck by lightning. The students did recover consciousness 'after a few hours', so you can judge for yourself whether to try this at home next time someone you know is struck and there is a ready supply of cow dung.

In the US state of Michigan, a burglar was arrested after raiding a house and crapping on the floor. At his trial the judge ordered Jonathan Naessens to clean 100 prison toilets.

Police in Teesside noticed a car being driven in a very erratic way, so they stopped the driver for questioning. Inside the car were 2,300 packets of Golden Virginia cigarette tobacco. Except the driver was either about to rip someone off or had been ripped off himself, because on closer examination each of the tobacco pouches contained camel shit.

UNUSUAL

Drivers went apeshit when two busy highways in the US city of Milwaukee had to be closed because a truck spilled its delightfully fragrant load of monkey faeces. The excrement, mixed with algae from the moat from which it had been dredged up in a standard monkey-shit clean-up operation at Milwaukee Zoo, was being transported for disposal when a latch broke on the truck's holding tank, and the liquid spewed out over the road. A zoo spokesperson described the smell as: 'On a scale of one to ten – a nine.'

In Walthamstow, in London, workers were clearing a drain blockage in the street outside the house of Terri Reynolds. When the jetting hose was directed up the wrong pipe, the toilet in Terri's house exploded with such force that excrement was splattered over the bathroom walls and ceiling and outside onto the landing walls and carpet. Looking on the bright side, no one was sitting on the toilet at the time.

SEEPING TOILETS

It would seem to be the birthright of a Texan – to strike oil on their ranch, or even in their back garden. But when Leila LeTourneau of Longview came home from work one evening to find crude oil flowing round her house, her first impression was not that she had struck it rich. Especially since the oil was coming up through her toilet. The theory was that her house had been built over an abandoned but poorly plugged oil well.

A city centre superloo went haywire and blew its own roof off in Stoke-on-Trent. The electronically controlled toilet had a surge of water the wrong way up its back passage, which caused an explosion powerful enough to rip off the roof and damage the pavement. No one was inside, fortunately, otherwise they would never have been able to prove it was a fault and not their toilet habits that blew the roof off.

SORRY ABOUT THE DELAY

A bank statement was sent out from Westpac Bank to the Boomerang Fashion Store, just over the road in Kerikeri, on the North Island of New Zealand. But it took

A history book, appropriately enough, made its way back to a library in Malta after 42 years. Ernie Roscouet, a former RAF squaddie in Malta, went home to the Channel Islands in June 1962, having inadvertently packed a library book. Forty-two years later, his wife gave him a holiday to Malta as his 65th birthday present, and he took advantage of the trip to return the book. Mr Roscouet said, 'It's been on my conscience all this time.' He expected a hefty fine, but instead was rewarded for his honesty with a nice cup of coffee.

a little while to get there, because it went first to Christchurch, on the South Island, then back north to Auckland and then to Singapore. From Singapore it carried on its Kiwi flight to Germany, then Austria, before arriving just over the road at the shop. That plucky little bank statement. Disney should make a film about it.

LACK OF HARMONY

Amid great fanfare, an eternal flame was lit on Millennium Eve in the city of Birmingham, with the aim of promoting world peace and harmony. No surprises

chinese record

In a Las Vegas casino the world record for Chinese whispers was set, when 614 people transmitted a whispered message. It was set off by comedian Mac King, who whispered 'Mac King is a comedy genius', which ended up, 613 sets of ears later, as 'Macaroni cantaloupe knows the future.'

then that last year it was extinguished in a sordid dispute over who pays the gas bill. The 33-foot-high sculpture was a gift to the Birmingham City Council from a coalition of Christian churches in the region and costs £12,000 a year to run. At first it was sponsored by a smoke alarm company, but when the sponsorship expired the City Council decided that the price of eternal peace and world harmony was a little too steep. They said they preferred a flame-effect electric light, and that the gas flame even contributes to global warming.

HOME SWEET HOME

Workers at a rubbish dump in Berlin were investigating the mystery of why fireworks had been set off at the dump, and discovered that a man had been living there for a whole decade. The 51-year-old man, named as

Harald, had dug out a three-foot-high living area deep inside the rubbish, furnishing it over time with a mattress, shelves and a cupboard. Harald lived a nocturnal existence, sleeping in his shelter during the day and wandering the tip at night in search of food, which he warmed over candles, and water, which he got from a tank at the staff office. Harald could have gone on living inside the dump undisturbed, since the staff had no idea he was there. The fireworks were set off by him, in an attempt to draw attention to his sad, lonely plight.

Not True, Unfortunately

We round off the collection of weird-but-true (as far as we know!) stories with a few weird-but-untrue ones.

A story that arrived in my inbox one day from a friend seemed interesting – but just a little too good to be true. Here's the story:

Bosses of a publishing firm are trying to work out why no one noticed that one of their employees had been sitting dead at his desk for *five days* before anyone asked if he was feeling OK. George Turklebaum, 51, who had been employed as a proofreader at a New York firm for 30 years, had a heart attack in the open-plan office he shared with 23 other workers. He quietly passed away on Monday, but nobody noticed until Saturday morning when an office cleaner asked why he was still working during the weekend.

His boss Elliot Wachiaski said: 'George was always the first guy in each morning and the last to leave at night – so no one found it unusual that he was in the same position all that time and didn't say anything. He was always absorbed in his work and kept much to himself.' A post-mortem examination revealed that he had been dead for five days after suffering a coronary. Ironically, George was proofreading manuscripts of medical textbooks when he died.

A nice touch was that this story arrived inside a graphic of a coffin, but alas that didn't make it any more true. This urban myth first appeared around three years ago, and also exists in a version featuring a geologist instead of a proof-

Another story that was swiftly quashed as being nothing more than a rumour came out of Iran. Officials in the city of Khomein were forced to deny the quickly spreading story that 14 male dwarfs were living in the citadel, living exclusively on macaroni and speaking only at the time of the call to prayer. Local tradition has it that dwarfs are similar to djinns (wicked spirits), and it was thought that the rumour was nothing more than an attempt to drive down property prices around the citadel! What the macaroni had to do with it, we cannot say. But it's pasta joke.

reader. The dead (sorry about the pun) giveaway is the simple detail that in reality a corpse begins to bloat and stink and decompose and leak revolting fluids in less than five days; the idea that no one would notice the stench of a dead body in a nice clean office is inconceivable. But it's a nice metaphor for the impersonal and detached way in which office life is led.

Another story that found its way to me through cyberspace was this one. The headline read WANTED FOR ATTEMPTED MURDER, but the story that followed was not very clearly linked to the headline – always a warning signal that the story may be a wind-up. And although it was also to be found in a 'Strange But True' story section, it most definitely is not true.

Linda Burnett, 23, was visiting her in-laws, and while there went to a nearby supermarket to pick up some groceries. Several people noticed her sitting in her car with the windows rolled up and with her eyes closed, with both hands behind her head.

One customer who had been at the store for a while became concerned and walked over to the car. He noticed that Linda's eyes were now open, and she looked very strange. He asked her if she was OK, and Linda replied that she'd been shot in the back of the head, and had been holding her brains in for over an hour.

The man called the paramedics, who broke into the car because the doors were locked and Linda refused to remove her hands from her head. When they finally got in, they found that Linda had a wad of bread dough on the back of her head.

A Pillsbury biscuit canister had exploded from the heat, making a loud noise that sounded like a gunshot, and the wad of dough had hit her in the back of her head. When she reached back to find out what it was, she felt the dough and thought it was her brains. She initially passed out, but quickly recovered and tried to hold her brains in for over an hour. And, yes, Linda is a blonde.